A FEDERATION FOR
WESTERN EUROPE

A FEDERATION FOR
WESTERN EUROPE

by

W. IVOR JENNINGS
M.A., LL.D.

*Reader in English Law in the University
of London
Of Gray's Inn, Barrister-at-Law*

*CAMBRIDGE
AT THE UNIVERSITY PRESS*

1940

CAMBRIDGE
UNIVERSITY PRESS

University Printing House, Cambridge CB2 8BS, United Kingdom

Cambridge University Press is part of the University of Cambridge.

It furthers the University's mission by disseminating knowledge in the pursuit of
education, learning and research at the highest international levels of excellence.

www.cambridge.org
Information on this title: www.cambridge.org/9781316612903

© Cambridge University Press 1940

First published 1940
First paperback edition 2016

A catalogue record for this publication is available from the British Library

ISBN 978-1-316-61290-3 Paperback

CONTENTS

PREFACE

ADVOCATES of a federal solution of our immediate post-war problems have been accused of favouring a vague Utopian ideal without giving adequate consideration to the many difficulties involved. In a recent issue of *The Spectator*, for instance, Mr Harold Nicolson expresses the hope "that the Federal Unionists will not allow their flock to imagine that they have discovered a solution when in fact they have done no more than propound a most important riddle". The criticism was no doubt just according to the information possessed by Mr Nicolson and others outside FEDERAL UNION. In fact, however, those connected with that organisation have for a long time realised that a general idea is not a solution, and committees called together by Mr Patrick Ransome and presided over by Sir William Beveridge have been at work for months on the detailed problems involved. Mr Nicolson mentions, for instance, a number of specific difficulties which, he thought, ought to have been discussed. I have personally been present when every one of those difficulties has been debated at length. Indeed, we could add hundreds to the score that Mr Nicolson mentions. I was asked to attend a meeting of the Political Committee immediately on my return from Canada in October. After that, it was thought desirable that a constitutional lawyer should be present at the meetings of the various groups of experts. As a result, I have been present at every meeting, with the exception of the first meeting of the Economics Committee. The experts present at these meetings have been drawn from the best talent avail able outside the Government service, and many of them have doubted the practicability of federation as a solution but have nevertheless given us their assistance on technical problems. In consequence, I have had every opportunity of formulating tentative conclusions.

The problems involved cannot be settled, even to our own satisfaction, in a few months. In particular, FEDERAL UNION itself cannot make up its mind on the details of its proposals without much more discussion, not only among experts in Great Britain, but also among experts elsewhere. Plans have already been formed for beginning this process of wider consultation. We have, however, reached the stage in which individual members are seeing the trees as well as the wood. Moreover, while we are debating the planting of the trees we must remember the nature of the wood. It is, for instance, useless for the economists to reach conclusions which the political scientists have pronounced to be politically impracticable. Accordingly, with the consent of Sir William Beveridge and Mr Ransome, I decided that it was desirable for me to produce a tentative plan which would enable the various groups of experts to see in what context their own conclusions might have to be placed and which would at the same time enable the public generally to give us more effective criticism of our work.

It follows that the plan discussed in this book is not FEDERAL UNION's plan. It is published under my name and I take sole responsibility. For that reason I have avoided the editorial "we" and, since I dislike intensely what may be called "the lawyer's passive" in such phrases as "it is submitted that", I have been compelled to appear personally in the text more frequently than I should normally desire. This plan could not, however, have been produced without the assistance of many who are far better qualified to deal with the issues. Their assistance has been fundamental. On the other hand, it has not always been conclusive. Where alternatives have been suggested, I have chosen that which appeared to me, on reflection, to be the best. Many questions discussed in the text have never been submitted to expert opinion and all are still under discussion. The plan is, therefore, essentially personal and tentative. It is very rough and immature, and it is published only because we are anxious to meet the widest and most intense barrage of criticism that we can. No body of experts sitting in the cloistered seclusion of an Oxford College can by themselves produce a scheme which will prove acceptable to two hundred millions of people. Still less can a single constitutional lawyer, travelling between the London School of Economics in Cambridge and the London School of Economics still in London, hope to dictate to twelve democracies and an enemy dictatorship. What we hope

is that large numbers of people, in FEDERAL UNION'S
local study groups and outside, in England and abroad,
will rend this plan to tatters and piece together something infinitely better.

I realise that every question raised needs to be debated
at much greater length. My aim was, however, to produce not a learned treatise but an elementary and short
exposition which would enable people unfamiliar with
the technicalities to take part in the discussion. If I had
been writing for experts I should have avoided some
subjects, such as the economic questions, altogether. On
the other hand, I should have prepared a documented
and technical argument on the purely constitutional
issues which might have been more persuasive for the
expert but unintelligible to the layman. I hope, too,
that I shall not be taken to be speaking for FEDERAL
UNION. Though I have collaborated in their research
work, I have taken no part in their organisation, and
I have no more authority to pledge them than I have
to pledge the League of Nations. Members of FEDERAL
UNION who dislike my conclusions need not withdraw
their membership. I shall, no doubt, alter my own
opinion many times, and it is extremely unlikely that
FEDERAL UNION would adopt this plan—indeed, I do
not even know whether it is the intention of the organisation to produce a detailed plan. For the same reason,
it is unnecessary that persons who are not members of
FEDERAL UNION, who accept the general idea of
federation, but who disagree with me, should refrain
from joining. A statement of principles in half a page

can be obtained from 44, Gordon Square, London,
W.C. 1. All this means only that the faults in this
book are due entirely to my own ignorance and in-
experience.

W. IVOR JENNINGS

33 *Clarence Road*
  St Albans

CHAPTER I

THE PURPOSES OF FEDERATION

§ 1. Towards a Practicable Scheme.

The desirability of replacing international anarchy by
international government is so generally recognised in
Great Britain that it needs no demonstration. Those
who have given thought to the problems of international
relations have asserted for generations that "ultimately"
sovereign states must be replaced by world order. Even
now that "ultimately" is remote. It is clear enough
that the difficulties of bringing China, Japan, India, the
Soviet Union and the American continent into some
form of world government closer than the League of
Nations are insuperable. The League of Nations involved
too close a relationship to secure the support of the
United States of America. There is nothing to suggest
that the events of twenty years have made closer international control more practicable. On the contrary,
that period has seen a deterioration of world conditions
which makes it doubtful if even the League of Nations
can become world-wide in its scope within a short time.
We cannot, however, leave the conditions of 1939 to
continue, and it is wise to make an attempt to solve the
most immediate of our problems, and in particular those
which gave rise to the present European war. The
proposition on which this book is founded is that a large

number of the difficulties which vex the world can be solved by the establishment of a democratic federation in Western Europe.

The practicability of this proposal depends on two factors. It depends in the first instance on persuading the nations to send representatives to an international conference with instructions to prepare a constitution. To make this step possible, it is necessary to persuade public opinion in the several countries that the step is urgent and essential. In part, such persuasion depends upon the second factor, which is the possibility of providing a constitution which does not demand too great a sacrifice from the federating states, which does however solve the major European problems, and which will work when it is established. Though the form of government would be the concern of statesmen and not of propagandists, the people are not likely to urge a proposal upon their leaders unless they are given a reasonably precise notion of what it would imply.

It is not my purpose in this book to undertake the task of persuasion. Mr Streit in *Union Now* and Mr Curry in *The Case for Federal Union* have already covered the ground. My task is directed rather towards the second factor, the feasibility of federation as a working system. This book is, therefore, an attempt to consider the difficulties which would have to be faced if the statesmen of Western Europe found themselves charged with the task of drafting a federal constitution. My aim is propagandist in the sense that I am anxious to show that federation will work so as to persuade the reader to support the proposal. At the same time, I propose to consider the difficulties frankly, and in so doing I may induce some readers to believe that federation is not practicable, that the difficulties really are too great, and that nations cannot be expected to surrender so much authority.

"Federation" is not a magic formula. It is nothing more than the name of a complicated system of government which nobody would wish to see established anywhere if he could think of a better. There are vast difficulties to be faced, and easy optimism is almost as dangerous as the still easier pessimism. Moreover, democracies must not in connection with foreign policy advocate a vague Utopianism based upon empty sentiments and inadequate understanding of the problems involved. Nothing is more dangerous than an impracticable ideal, and more particularly an ideal which involves the collaboration of someone else who does not support it. My task is to consider the difficulties and if, in doing so, I persuade some readers that the scheme is impracticable, some service will have been done. If, however, I provide reasonable solutions for the difficulties, I hope that the reader will be persuaded of the practicability of federation.

I have gone so far as to draft a Constitution. Its primary purpose was not for publication at all, but simply to make my own ideas definite and to secure the criticisms of those whose opinions I value. Nothing is easier than to accept general principles without understanding them. In the discussions which I have attended during the past months, I have frequently heard expounded, and have myself expounded, bright ideas which appeared futile and even ridiculous as soon as I attempted to give them the precision of a legal draft. My draft does nothing more than provide possible solutions for difficulties which I foresee. It is published only because it may provide a basis of discussion for others. It has already served that purpose. The first rough draft was provided not by me but by two authorities on federal constitutions. It was debated at length by a group of instructed men. Its ideas were criticised, modified, elaborated. Other groups discussed other aspects of the problem, especially the economic and the colonial. I was present at nearly all those discussions, and my draft is the immediate result. It represents my views only, but my views as modified by the persuasion of authorities for whose opinions I have the greatest respect. We found a truly amazing measure of agreement (even among economists!), but where we differed I have inserted my own opinion for purposes of discussion. I do not assert that my solutions are better than theirs; I merely think that they are better.

Nor do I suggest that, if federation is achieved, the constitution will be anything like my draft. The process of securing agreement is a process of compromise among widely different views. The Senate of the United States of America, for instance, was a compromise between those who wanted membership of the House of Representatives to be based on population and those who wanted it to be based on equality of states. The acceptance of one compromise, moreover, changes the aspect of other difficulties—the acceptance of the principle of equality in the United States Senate enabled the smaller states, who had opposed wide federal powers, to make and support proposals for increased powers. My purpose is to provide a basis for wide unofficial discussion.

If the result is to convince instructed public opinion that a federation is possible, my aim will be attained. Public opinion, if strong and vocal enough, can induce naturally hesitant statesmen to find a solution. I repeat, though, that I am not writing as a propagandist. I am concerned more with the practicability of working a federal system than with the practicability of achieving a federal system. In this latter connection I would add one remark only. I have heard many people say that, though they personally are perfectly prepared, for instance, for the transference of the British Navy to federal control, they are perfectly certain that there will be general opposition. If I ask for particulars as to persons and classes, I receive positive answers; but when I ask those persons and representatives of those classes whether *they* are prepared to hand over the British Navy, they reply that they are quite prepared for it, but that "other people" are not. These "other people" prove to belong to those groups to which I had spoken in the first instance. It may be, of course, that I am not being given truthful answers, and that they are all passing on a responsibility for opposition which they hesitate to assume. I think, however, that the element of agreement is much greater than most individuals imagine. It is very likely that the same process is being followed in other countries and, more than that, between other countries. If we could find out what reactions German citizens would make to a proposal for federation, we should probably find that they would say that, though they would be fully prepared to see the German Army, as such, disappear, they are "absolutely certain" that the British Navy would be retained by us. If this is so, the task of securing agreement is much easier than it appears to be. If we are agreed that "ultimately" federation is desirable, we can probably agree that it is desirable within the next few years.

§ 2. Federation or War.

Europe is the cauldron in which most wars are brewed. There have been, of course, many wars elsewhere, but if we can solve the European question we shall take a step forward of untold value. Not only should we prevent wars in Europe, but also we should prevent European rivalry from leading to war elsewhere. Moreover, the Federation which is proposed in this book would be so strong that threats against the security of its outlying portions—in the Far East or North Africa, for instance—dare not be made. At the same time it would be, I think, a peaceful federation which involved no threat against an extra-European power.

If we could prevent wars everywhere we should, of course, produce an even greater benefit to humanity. We could not, however, propose at this stage a practicable form of international government. It is certain that Japan would not withdraw from China at once, and equally certain that the rest of the world would not consent to the stabilisation of the present position in the Far East. It is reasonable to infer that if the United States of America would not accept the feeble obligations of the Covenant of the League of Nations, she would not accept a scheme which involved an even further intervention by her in the affairs of the world at large. Moreover, the task of providing a representative government for the illiterate millions of Asia and Africa is too vast, and a world system of government would be too enormous for our present political technique. It is still true that "ultimately" we must have world government, but before that aim is achieved we must equate more closely the civilisations of the East and of the West, raise the standard of living and education in Asia and Africa, and develop closer communication between the continents.

The first step to this solution clearly lies in the development of the League of Nations. No doubt the obligations of the Covenant require strengthening; and if they are strengthened such breaches as the Japanese attack on China will be less easy. Moreover, if the main problems of Europe could cease to be League problems, the task of the League would be immeasurably eased. It was in Europe that the League system of preventing war finally broke down. The real task of the League is, however, not so much prevention of war as the development of such conditions that world government becomes possible. The prevention of war has been the most urgent problem for the past twenty years and has therefore received most attention. Regarded with a historical perspective, however, the most important part of the League's work has been the part which it has played supremely well, the part which is concerned with economic rehabilitation and co-operation, with the control of the drug traffic and traffic in women, with international action for the prevention and eradication of disease, and with intellectual co-operation.

These functions will receive due emphasis if we, the people of Europe, can solve our own political problems without burdening the League machinery any longer. Twenty years' experience has shown that these problems require a much stronger organisation and a much more emphatic co-operation than the League machinery, designed as it was for world-wide collaboration, rendered or can render possible. There was something to be said for the lack of interest sometimes displayed by South American states; there was also something to be said for the attitude of the Republican Party in the United States of America, unfortunate though the sequel proved to be. Collaboration from both parts of the American continent will be readily forthcoming if we show that we, in Europe, are not asking for outside support in our own disputes, but are asking the American peoples to give us assistance in making a better and more civilised world.

Those of us who believe in the federal solution are not, therefore, opponents of the League of Nations. Many of the most fervent "federalists" are also among the most fervent supporters of the League. We believe not that our proposal tends to destroy the League ideal, but that it will help immeasurably to make it more easily realisable. If we can make war in Western Europe absolutely impossible and if, as I shall suggest we can, we can make war in Europe virtually impossible, three-quarters of the League's task in preventing war will be accomplished; and if Western Europe comes to Geneva as a unit, the problems to be solved in Geneva will be fewer and much more easily solved. Let us, then, remember the whole range of world problems, but direct our attention primarily to Europe.

Conditions in Europe change rapidly. Ten years ago the prospect of the rapid emergence of Germany as an aggressive power appeared remote. Whatever the de-merits of the Soviet system were, few would have said two years ago that it would embark on a policy of imperialist expansion. The possibility that some other state of Europe, perhaps even our own, will adopt a policy of forceful domination under the control of some ambitious adventurer cannot be kept out of considera-tion. "Sanctions" are of little use because some states, often small neighbours of the aggressor, dare not impose them; other states decide not to impose them because they see the possibility of capturing trade; still others are not bound to impose sanctions at all. The use of armed force by such an international organisation as the League of Nations leads to war if the aggressive nation feels strong enough to defy it.

Disarmament is not a practicable proposal. Great

Britain cannot disarm so long as Japan does not. Germany cannot disarm, or safely be disarmed, so long as the Soviet Union does not. Few would accept an alleged disarmament by the Soviet Union as being a disarmament in fact; and in any case Russia cannot and will not disarm so long as Japan does not. Hitler has shown, too, that secret rearmament is possible and open rearmament in breach of treaty practicable so long as Europe is divided. All the European powers have ratified the Protocol of 1925 against gas warfare, yet all those nations have supplies of gas ready for use if necessary, and all have supplies of gas-masks, believing that the enemy will use gas. If disarmament were provided for, every nation would either rearm secretly or provide the means for a rapid expansion of its armaments.

The alternatives, therefore, are war once in every generation or federation. War within a federation is, in modern times, practically impossible. Modern warfare is a highly complex and technical process requiring not only mechanical armaments, but also highly trained mechanics and a whole apparatus of industrial preparation for war. The example of the Civil War in the United States, which causes many prospective "federalists" to hesitate, is irrelevant. It would no longer be possible for the Southern States to wage war against the United States, because spirited and patriotic men, mounted on horseback and armed with rifles, are no match for a modern army. Civil war to-day, in a highly organised state with an adequate defence force, is an impossibility so long as the army holds together and obeys orders.

The problem of preventing war in a federation, therefore, is not a highly complicated problem of the kind that the League of Nations has had to face: it is a simple problem of administrative technique, and involves only the maintenance of the morale and the discipline of the armed forces.

It is therefore a primary purpose of the Federation proposed in this book to prevent war in Western Europe. A federation which included Germany, France and the United Kingdom would include the major participants in the three major wars of the past sixty years. It would, however, do far more. It would prevent war elsewhere in Europe. The federal force would be by far the most powerful in the world. Being maintained by a democratic system interested only in the maintenance of peace and having no anxiety for more territory, colonial or otherwise, it would not be an instrument of aggression. On the contrary, it would be strong enough to prevent aggression elsewhere in Europe. The Concert of Europe worked well enough after 1815 so long as it was a concert. The great powers in unison can prevent aggression outside and compel resort to peaceful settlement. No nation, not even an imperialist Russia, would dare to go to war if a great Western European power said nay and meant it. The proposals of this book are restricted to a federation of Western Europe for reasons given in the next chapter. It is hoped, however, that the extension of democracy and the economic and cultural development of Europe would permit its gradual extension so as to include the whole of Europe and, perhaps, the whole of the world. In the meantime, the Federation would not only establish permanent peace in Western Europe; it would also compel permanent peace elsewhere in Europe.

The primary purpose of federation, then, is the perpetuation of European peace. For this purpose the Federation itself must have complete powers over defence, internal and external. It must, also, be the body conducting foreign affairs, represented in the League of Nations, negotiating with other powers, preventing other powers in Europe, by the inherent strength of its war potential and the instrumentality of the League of Nations, from breaking the peace.

§ 3. Economic Relations and Colonies.

That is not all. A federation cannot be built on negative principles. The causes of dissension do not lie only in the extravagant nationalism that ambitious kings and reckless leaders foster for their own ends, and sycophantic professors develop to please them. There are grave economic problems for which solutions must be found. The authors of the Treaties of Versailles and St Germain, in their anxiety to give freedom to oppressed peoples, created greater problems than they solved. They split Austria-Hungary, which had been an economic unit, into fragments, each of which followed the example of the rest of Europe in creating barriers against trade and migration. Poland, too, was severed from its former connections. All this was no doubt necessary and desirable on political grounds, but no adequate restrictions were imposed on economic grounds. Self-determination, like patriotism, is not enough. The successive post-war depressions resulted in a chaos which Europe and the world cannot afford to see repeated—a chaos to which all the nations of the world, including Great Britain and the United States, contributed. More than any other single factor it was the cause of the reversion to barbarism in Europe. But for the inflation in Germany, Hitler would have remained an obscure mountebank and the Nazi Party a comic minority.

Europe has, it is to be hoped, learned the lesson of 1931 as well as the lesson of 1939. The nations are economically inter-dependent, and the state that upsets the equilibrium for short-term advantages loses heavily in the long run. The economic rehabilitation of Western Europe will be the main tasks of post-war statesmen. Western Europe, at least, should be an economic unit at the earliest possible moment.

The problem of colonies is partly economic and partly purely political. Until 1932 it could be truly said that Great Britain obtained no economic advantage from her colonies which other nations could not obtain, subject only to the natural preference which British people have for British goods where they are equally cheap and equally good. Other nations have never, and Great Britain since 1932 has not, followed this practice. It may be that Adam Smith was right in saying that trade restrictions in and for colonies are disadvantageous to the nation that employs them—a mere constitutional lawyer can express no opinion on such controversies—

but what is certain is that they have been disadvantageous to other nations and to the colonies themselves. There is reasonable cause for complaint in the possession and economic exploitation of colonies and other dependencies by the "satisfied" nations who happened to be foremost in the scramble. Germany had particular cause for complaint in that such colonies as she had been able to obtain were taken from her in and before 1919. We could not expect her to enter a federation without some reasonable arrangement to meet this difficulty.

Probably, however, the economic motive is here less important than the purely political motive. There is satisfaction to some forms of national pride in contemplating the areas marked red on a map of the world. British and French people can emigrate without losing their nationality. Germans, and, in some degree, Italians, must live under an alien flag and speak an alien language. It is questionable whether emigration is necessary, and German and Italian practice has been in conflict with their protestations. It is nevertheless true that the possession of colonies by Great Britain, France, Holland and Portugal has been a source of real or manufactured dissatisfaction, and that the problem is one that must be discussed in relation to proposals for federation.

§ 4.   Plan of the Federation.

The Federation must, then, have powers over defence and foreign affairs, and some control over economic relations and colonies. The plans which might be developed for these purposes are numerous, and everything would depend on the conditions in which the proposal would become one of immediate and practical concern. The nature of the problems involved becomes clear, however, if we accept a plan as a basis for discussion, examine the reasons which induce us to accept that plan, and debate the possible alternatives. The plan which I have adopted is to be found in the Appendix to this book. The reasons and the alternatives are to be found in subsequent chapters, each of which takes up one item in the plan. The early chapters discuss the organisation considered desirable to carry out the purposes mentioned above; the later chapters discuss what the powers should be to carry out the purposes.

CHAPTER II

A DEMOCRATIC FEDERATION

§ 1. The Nucleus.

The limits of the Federation, if it were formed at all, would depend in the first place upon the nations who could be persuaded to join. That obvious fact does not, however, dispense with the necessity for considering what nations should be asked to join. If it were merely a question of obtaining the most convenient area for the prevention of war, the conduct of foreign relations, and the solution of economic difficulties, the answer would obviously include all the nations of Europe, except possibly the primarily Asiatic nations (in a geographical sense) of Turkey and the Soviet Union.

Technical considerations suggest, however, that the initial aim should be more limited. A federal system implies the division of governmental powers into two classes, federal powers exercised by the federal institutions, and State powers exercised by the institutions of the several States. In respect of the services for which the federal institutions are responsible, they have direct contact with the people and not an indirect contact through the States. If the armed forces are controlled by the Federation, they are enlisted directly by the Federal Government and not provided by the States. If powers are given to the Federal Legislature the laws which it passes apply immediately to the people and are enforced, where necessary, without the intervention of the State authorities.

It is not impossible to imagine a dictatorial federation. Indeed, some of the South American federal republics have at times approximated to this system, though they have then been more dictatorial than federative. It is clear, however, that the democratic nations of Western Europe would not enter a federation that was not democratic. Indeed, it is a main purpose of federal proposals to maintain democratic institutions in Europe. The Federal Legislature must, therefore, be an elected body; and if it is to be federal it must contain at least one House elected by the people at large. Elections are futile unless they are free elections. They require a complex of rules which are sometimes referred to as "fundamental liberties", and are sometimes embodied in declarations of rights like the American Bill of Rights and the French Declaration of the Rights of Man. It must be possible to form parties, to have rival candidates proposing rival policies; there must be freedom of speech, freedom of public assembly, secret ballots, impartial and honest counting of votes. These things are not practicable in a dictatorial State. It is impossible to imagine that in Italy or Russia there could be a one-party totalitarian regime for the purpose of State elections and a free democratic system for federal elections. A party could not be suppressed for State purposes and encouraged for federal purposes, nor could opponents of the State regime be "liquidated" because of their State activities and acclaimed as representatives of the people because of their federal activities.

It is not the inevitable conclusion that totalitarian States must be excluded from the Federation. One would make many compromises in order to bring in Italy, Spain and Portugal. Their peoples have made immense contributions to the sum of Western culture. They have languages belonging to the same Latin group as the French. Being Catholic States, they would enable the relations between the Federation and the Papacy to be settled more easily. Their economic systems are closely linked with, and indeed are part of, the general economic system of Western Europe. Their inclusion would enable some of the political problems of the Mediterranean to be solved much more easily—particularly the problems caused by British and French (or federal) control of the entrances to that Sea.

If these States were brought in the solution would be to leave the method of election to the Federal Legislature to be determined by the States. The Italian representatives would then be, presumably, nominees of the Italian Government, the Chamber of Corporations, or the Fascist Party. These are alternative methods of stating exactly the same thing. Being a totalitarian State, the Government, the Chamber and the Party are merely different organisations expressing the same point of view. The Italian representatives would in different ways say the same thing. They would vote as a *bloc*, not according to any individual views that they might develop, but according to the views elaborated by their leader after consultation with the Duce.

It is, however, essential to the working of a democratic institution that voting should not take place in racial, religious, or national *blocs*. The democratic system works best where the two-party system operates in such a way that a slight change in public opinion produces a change in government. The Government then temporarily in power has to keep in accord with changes in public opinion lest it find at the next election that the Opposition has gained sufficient support to take power in its turn. Government and Opposition have to lead public opinion, but they also have to follow it. They appeal to the same minority of electors, the "floating vote" which may be large or small according to circumstances, but which, whatever its size, really determines the results of elections and, therefore, the actions of Governments.

It is indeed essential for the successful operation of a federation that representatives should not vote on national lines. We have had experience in Great Britain of an Irish Party which voted solidly as a *bloc* and solely on Irish considerations. If the House of Commons had been composed of representatives of England, Wales, Scotland and Ireland who voted and thought as such, the British Constitution would long since have broken down. The Swiss Constitution has been supremely successful only because the representatives of the cantons think of themselves primarily as Swiss, and do not vote solely according to canton, language or religion. The great fear of Canada, fortunately avoided by the per-

spicacity of leaders like Sir John Macdonald and Sir
Wilfrid Laurier, has been a split between the English-
speaking Provinces and French-speaking Quebec. The
difficulties in Belgium in recent times have been due
primarily to the tendency of the Flemings to think of
themselves mainly as Flemings and not as Belgians. Our
difficulties in Palestine, in India and in Ceylon have
been due to the fear that Jews and Arabs, Hindus and
Mohammedans, Sinhalese and Tamils, would vote as
such and provide no basis for effective collaboration.
The Constitution of Malta was suspended because the
conflict of parties became a conflict of Maltese-speaking
and Italian-speaking groups.

Examples are legion, and they all lead to the conclusion that the democratic system works only where
the same person may have different opinions, and therefore vote for different persons, at different times. A
federation in particular will completely break down if
each of its parts acts as a unit and not as part of the
whole. The idea of federation implies that the interests
of the parts are bound up in the interests of the whole.
Different views may be held of those interests and of the
means by which they are to be attained. The foreign
policy to be followed, the size of the armed forces, the
methods of taxation, the problems of tariffs, and many
more matters, are legitimate sources of differences of
opinion, about which people in a given political unit
ought to differ. We ought to have, and must have if the
system is to operate, party organisations cutting across
national boundaries. Mr Chamberlain is more likely to

agree with M. Daladier than with Mr Attlee; Mr Attlee is more likely to agree with the Swedish Social Democratic Party than with the British Conservative Party, just as Republicans in New York prefer Mr Hoover of Iowa to Mr Roosevelt of New York.

It is theoretically not impossible to have representatives holding different opinions sent to the Federal Legislature from the democratic countries and representatives holding the same opinions sent from totalitarian countries. As a system, however, it would be most difficult to operate. The Italian votes, for instance, would be cast as a *bloc* not according to the views of the representatives on the basis of federal issues and federal discussions, but according to the policy of the Italian Government. So far as Italy was concerned, the Federation would not be a federation, but a league of which Italy was a member. If the Federal Government wanted Italian support it would negotiate with the Italian Government. Other State Governments would take sides, and in large degree we should reproduce the conditions in the League of Nations, where decisions were taken in fact not in the Council or the Assembly, but in back-stairs negotiations leading, in the first part of its history, to formal League decisions, and in the later part to "four-power" and other decisions which completely ignored the League.

Indeed, the result of forming an Italian or Spanish or Portuguese *bloc* would probably be to form also British, French, German and other national *blocs*. If the States were empowered to choose their own method of representation there would be agitation for nomination by Governments to offset the advantage possessed by the totalitarian States through their manipulation of a single and unanimous body of representatives. In other words, the Federation would in fact be a league of States and not a federation of peoples.

§ 2. A League of States.

If we are to have a league of States it should be specifically so provided. Such a league is certainly easier to form than a federation of peoples. It is true that the world has never yet seen a successful league with direct powers of taxation and law-making and with control of armed forces and foreign policy. The Greek Leagues of Cities, the old Swiss Confederation, the Netherlands Union, the first United States of America, the League of Nations, all broke down or had to be converted into federations. History is, of course, an insecure guide, but the problem now before us is far more difficult than has ever been faced before. A Western European League or Confederation would be easier to operate than the League of Nations. It might be successful so long as the conditions which gave it birth continued. It would be better than the international anarchy into which Europe has again been thrown. If it is the alternative to the maintenance of full national sovereignty it is the better alternative. It would be too weak, however, to survive a crisis. It might split with a crash greater than any the world has yet seen. If the separate States kept armies, they would tend to consider them as possible instruments against other States in the Confederation. If the Confederation alone had armed forces, the constant emphasis upon separate national interests would prevent those forces from becoming internationalised in spirit. Civil war is always possible if armies split. It is most undesirable that cause should be given for the maintenance of distinct loyalties. The only real solution, in my opinion, is a democratic federation.

§ 3. A Federation of Democracies.

A democratic federation implies, then, a federation of democracies. Fortunately, democracy is distributed on a geographic basis in the north-west of Europe. Assuming a democratic Germany, there would then be a solid block of democratic States stretching from the Pyrenees, the Mediterranean and the Swiss and Austrian Alps to the Arctic Circle, a block comprising France, Germany, Switzerland, Luxemburg, Belgium, Holland, the United Kingdom, Eire, Denmark, Sweden, Finland, Norway and Iceland. Its boundaries on the East are at this stage uncertain. Austria might or might not choose to become part of a democratic Germany. The boundaries of Czechoslovakia, Poland and Finland will depend primarily on the results of wars now raging.

It is convenient to assume for the time being the exclusion of Czechoslovakia and Poland. We do not at present know that the Czechs, the Slovaks and the Ruthenians will decide to form a single state, nor the kind of government that would be set up. The eastern parts of Czechoslovakia contained a large illiterate population among which a democracy does not work well. Czechoslovakia is obviously the marginal case, to be dealt with in the light of post-war conditions. Its incorporation or non-incorporation is irrelevant for the major issues discussed in this book, and it will therefore be convenient to exclude it from consideration. Poland has never worked a democratic system effectively, and from the Pilsudski coup of 1926 until its absorption by Germany and Russia it was a dictatorship. It contained a vast illiterate population which had not reached the standards of living and education of the Western democracies. It is a little difficult to ask Polish peasants to think of themselves as citizens of a vast federation, though the experience of the United States has shown that they can be "democratised" in a different social and economic milieu in the course of two generations.

The comparatively small and compact group of thirteen democratic nations (including Germany as in March 1937) in the West contains, with their European dependencies, a population of 205 millions, or rather more than half the population of Europe and about half as much again as are to be found in the United States of America. Excluding Greenland, it occupies an area less than one-third of that of the United States of America or of Canada. Though its inhabitants speak at least ten different languages, these nearly all belong to two main language groups. Of the 205 million people, in fact, about 175 millions have English, French or German as their mother tongue. Secondary education having proceeded far, large sections of the populations understand two or even three of these languages. The thirteen States, too, include most of the great commercial and industrial nations of the world, they all have large urban populations, and those populations have a relatively high standard of living. They are connected by excellent transport facilities infinitely better than those possessed by the United States in 1787. Finally, except for Switzerland, which is accustomed to federation, and Germany, which had experience of responsible government from 1919 to 1933, they all possess remarkably similar constitutional systems based upon the principles of the British Constitution.

The task of operating a federation within this area is technically perfectly simple. The external dependencies of some of the countries, and especially of Great Britain, create considerable difficulties which must be left until Chapter IV. The language difficulty is substantial, but it could be worked out in practice. It would not be impossible to allow speeches in any language and to provide simultaneous translations in English, French and German, as is often done at international conferences. There remains only the fundamental difficulty —and I should not be disposed to minimise it—of the strong nationalistic sentiments of these thirteen States.

It is, of course, the existence of these strong nationalistic sentiments which is the primary cause of war. If, as many assert, economic motives were the dominant factor, federation would be an obvious solution; and if the temporary revulsion against war which always arises at the coming of peace could be used to overcome the

opposition of interested economic groups and the moment
seized to give economic control to a federation, those
groups would perforce have to bring their pressure to
bear on the Federation. They would, so to speak, become
federalists because they would come to the European
equivalent of Washington to ask for federal favours. I do
not think, however, that anyone can read *Mein Kampf*
and examine the course of events from 1933 to 1938
and still believe that economic motives played an important part in German aggression. If we want to put
down aggression we must put down extreme nationalism.
This is a task, however, of persuasion and propaganda.
The formation of a federation would be in itself such
a limitation of sovereignty and nationalism that it would
of necessity divert some of the nationalistic fervour into
more socially profitable channels. Of the nations suggested for inclusion in the Federation, only Germany
has been aggressive in recent years; and, on the assump-
tions we are making of a preliminary German defeat,
Germans would not be in a position for some years to
think of nationalist aggression, and the best of them
would in fact be engaged with customary German
thoroughness in making the federal constitution work.

It must be remembered, too, that certain sections of
opinion already have close international relations. This
is particularly true of the trade union movement and
the parties represented in the Socialist International.
It may reasonably be assumed that the socialist parties
of Western Europe would federate in order to try to
capture the federal machinery. Inevitably the opposition

to social democracy in the several States would find common action essential. We should, in fact, find the party system in early operation and cutting across State boundaries. We should have a Government and an Opposition in action. They would probably be coalitions, and it is unlikely that we should obtain the simplicity of the British or the American two-party system, but at least we should have a parliamentary system that could be worked.

The nationalistic difficulty is, I feel, more a difficulty of initiating the Federation than of working it when it is established. It is one of the advantages of the scope proposed that it would consist in large degree of peoples accustomed to the inevitable compromises of parliamentary and responsible government. One can surely say of the British people that they would find no great difficulty in finding elected representatives who would behave reasonably, who would think in European terms, and who would not wave the Union Jack as if it decided everything. Switzerland has shown that this habit of compromise is not a providential gift to the Anglo-Saxon peoples alone. Though a Frenchman may think that a good European is a good Frenchman, he also thinks that a good Frenchman is a good European—and French culture being what it is it does not matter much which way the statement is put. We are in fact proposing to extend to Europe the principles of 1789. The Germans have had few opportunities of producing good Europeans because their primary task was to produce good Germans and often, with German thoroughness, they pro-

duced them too good. Given the opportunity of working
in and for Europe, they would probably prove more
able than any. Finally, little need be said about the
smaller nations because it was part of their happy
circumstances before the war that they were good Europeans already.

§ 4.   The Admission of New States.

The question whether the Federation should be an
exclusive "aristocratic" Western European power or
whether it should be a nucleus for the further expansion
of international government is not, at this stage, fundamentally important. A constitutional convention would
not break down merely because some States were anxious
for extensions of area to be made easily while others
were anxious to make it more difficult. The question
would nevertheless be placed on the agenda and the
problem is one for discussion.

Most "federalists" start, like the present writer, from
the assumption that "ultimately" complete international
government will be necessary—not so much for the prevention of war as for the further development of economic
collaboration. For them, the answer to the question is
easy. While they would not be anxious for the admission
at an early stage of States whose problems were so
complicated that they added immeasurably to the difficulties of working a federal system, they would be anxious
to include as soon as possible contiguous States whose
problems were essentially the same as those of the
federated States. Among these, evidently, are Italy,

Spain and Portugal. One would hope, also, for a gradual extension into the south-east of Europe. The settlement of international problems of the first order through the creation of the Federation, the removal of the likelihood of aggression, and the general rise in the standard of living that federation would inevitably produce, would remove the main justification—if there be a justification—for the maintenance of dictatorial systems in the States outside the Federation. We should find, I think, a gradual extension of the democratic system in Europe, and a development of popular education among the more illiterate peoples of the Iberian Peninsula and the Balkans. It is therefore reasonable to contemplate a slow extension of the area of the Federation until it covered the whole of Europe, or at least that part of it which is outside the U.S.S.R.

Another consideration leads to the conclusion that Western Europe should regard itself as a nucleus for expansion and not an end in itself. We cannot anticipate what will be the position of the Soviet Union at the end of the present war. It is possible that it will be much stronger than it is at present. Its sphere of influence may extend over much of Eastern Europe. There is an obvious danger of conflict between the Federation and the Soviets which we must face. It is certainly not the intention of "federalists" to make the Federation an anti-Communist front. If that were the intention it would be impossible to form the Federation in the first instance. Truly democratic nations in modern conditions are not aggressive, and it would be one of the advantages of insisting on a democratic constitution as a condition of admission to the Federation that ambitious nationalistic fervour would be kept out. We can assume that a democratic Federation will not prove aggressive.

Whether Russia might not prove aggressive is a question much more difficult to answer. Until recently the answer which most would have given was that the Soviet weapon was not force but propaganda. The change in Soviet policy since the retirement of M. Litvinov has however caused many to proceed to the opposite conclusion. If that interpretation is correct—and at present I do not think that it is—the need for federation is all the more urgent as a defensive measure. Great Britain and France could not allow the Soviet Union to swallow up the nations of Europe one by one, for we should then get rid of Hitler only to be compelled to face Stalin. The Russians would not dare to attack a federation so powerful as that which we contemplate, or to develop aggressive designs in Eastern Europe if the West warned them off.

The condition of equilibrium between Eastern and Western Europe would nevertheless be somewhat unstable, and we must contemplate that at some time in the future the problem of admitting Russia into the Federation would have to be faced. If a democratic system of the Western type were created in the vast Russian dominions —and the rapid extension of education under the Soviet regime makes it less impracticable than it may appear at first sight—their admission on special terms would have to be contemplated.

This instance might suggest to many the desirability of making admission subject to stringent terms and conditions. It is clear, however, that no such stringency should be applied to democratic States in the Iberian Peninsula, Italy, or the Balkans. Moreover, there is another possibility which must not be left out of consideration. The inclusion of the United States of America at any stage of the proceedings would be most welcome. Though an application from the United States is most unlikely under present conditions, the formalities of entry should not be too complicated. The inclusion of the United States would, in fact, make the inclusion of a democratic Russia much easier because it would redress the balance of the enormous Russian population.*

Taking all these factors into consideration, I am in favour of easy admission so long as there is a reasonable measure of agreement within the Federation. The method depends in part on the composition of the Federal Legislature, but it will be seen from Article I, section 6, of the draft Constitution in the Appendix that I propose a two-thirds vote in each House. Some authorities wish to make admission somewhat more difficult by requiring also the consent of two-thirds of the States. It should be explained, however, that under

* According to current figures:

Western Europe	205	millions
U.S.S.R.	162	,,
Rest of Europe	84	,,
U.S.A.	137	,,
Total	588	millions

my scheme, if representatives voted according to States (which is unlikely) the consent of at least eleven of the eighteen States would be required. If the German representatives voted against, the consent of twelve States would be required; and if the United Kingdom and all the Dominion voted against, the incorporation of a new State would be impossible—but it is of course wildly improbable that all the United Kingdom and all the Dominion representatives would vote the same way.

§ 5. Collaboration with Other States.

The exclusion of non-democratic States does not necessarily imply that some advantages of the Federation could not be extended to them or that the Federation could not secure the benefit of their more limited collaboration. Spain and Portugal, and perhaps even Italy, might desire to enter the customs union which would be, according to my plan, one of the great advantages of the Federation. The fact that there were some elements, at least, of collaboration in Africa might induce Italy and Portugal to join for colonial purposes. Some States outside the Federation—Poland and Czechoslovakia, for instance—might undertake to maintain no armed forces if the Federation undertook their defence. These are examples of possibilities: they are not exhaustive, and they do not necessarily imply that collaboration would be sought or that satisfactory terms could be agreed upon.

There is, however, a distinct possibility that some such

arrangement could be made, and the Constitution should provide accordingly. Since the circumstances in which it would apply cannot be foreseen, the provision should be in very general terms. Accordingly, I have provided in Article I, section 7, of the draft for the application of any of the terms of the Constitution to a non-federated State, by a law passed by two-thirds of the members of each House. If such arrangements were made, it would also be desirable to include representatives of the State concerned in the Federal Legislature, though without a right to vote. The particular provision depends on the composition of the Federal Legislature, but my suggestion is contained in Article X, section 3.

CHAPTER III

THE BRITISH COMMONWEALTH
OF NATIONS

§ 1. Consequences of Federation.

The peculiarities of the British Commonwealth of Nations necessarily create difficulties in the formation and operation of any international organisation. Any proposal which did not take account of those peculiarities would be futile; and any proposal leading to the breaking up of the Commonwealth would not be acceptable to the British peoples. It should be emphasised at the outset that there is nothing in any proposal for federation, and certainly nothing in the proposals in this book, which infringes the position of the King or interferes with his relations with his dominions. British subjects would remain British subjects; the relations between the King and his several Governments would remain unimpaired. The Statute of Westminster of 1931 would not be amended even by the omission of a comma.

In practice, however, the proposals in this book would affect the relations between the nations of the Commonwealth in several ways and, though they assume knowledge of matters developed in later chapters, it will be convenient to set them out here.

1. The transfer of the general powers of defence to the Federation would prevent the United Kingdom from

carrying out its moral obligation to defend the Dominions against external aggression.

2. As the law stands at present, a declaration of war by the King implicates all parts of the British Empire except the Union of South Africa and Eire. In respect of any part of the British Commonwealth included in the Federation the King would no longer have power to declare war. If the Federation were at war, members of the British Commonwealth not part of the Federation would be neutral unless the King declared war on the advice of the respective Dominion Governments.

3. British subjects belonging to parts of the Commonwealth included in the Federation would remain British subjects, but would become also federal citizens. As the law now stands, however, the citizens or nationals of a Dominion are also British subjects (except that for the purposes of the law of Eire—but not for the purposes of English law—Irish citizens are not British subjects).

4. Immigration into and emigration from the Federation would, in due course, come under the control of the Federation and so the freedom of entry into and departure from the United Kingdom which is now possessed by all British subjects might disappear.

5. The Ottawa Agreements and other arrangements for Imperial preference would either be revoked or be extended to all members of the Federation.

§ 2. Inclusion in the Federation.

These difficulties would not arise if the Dominions— the position of India is considered below—became members of the Federation. In this respect Eire (for once) causes no complications. It is a European nation, and its inclusion would be welcomed on the same terms as other European nations. Its relations with the United

Kingdom under the Statute of Westminster, 1931, and the Executive Authority (External Relations) Act, 1936, would remain unaltered except so far as the latter dealt with functions transferred to the Federation.

There are reasons other than the difficulties already mentioned for welcoming the inclusion of the other Dominions in the Federation. Canada, Australia, South Africa and New Zealand are, in respect of population, small nations. They have together about 21 million white inhabitants, or about the same number as the Netherlands, Denmark, Sweden and Norway together. One of the difficulties of the Federation proposed is that about three-quarters of the European population would be found in three States only, Germany, the United Kingdom, and France. It is extremely unlikely that on any particular issue the votes from these three States would be cast as a *bloc*. The experience of the United States has been that fears by the small States of a combination among the larger States were groundless. The three countries would be represented by different party groups which would be unlikely to vote together. It is probable that votes would be cast rather according to economic interests than according to size. Moreover, the proposal to establish a second Chamber with weighted representation would give the smaller States a check on the power of the larger States. The difficulty is therefore not very great. It would nevertheless be an advantage to increase the number of smaller States so as to provide more balance within the Federation. It would, also, enable the Federation to realise that it was the nucleus of a world State. Presumably other European States have had enough experience of the working of the League of Nations to realise that giving representation to the Dominions does not, as was alleged in the United States in 1919, give extra votes to the United Kingdom.

From the point of view of the Dominions, there are even greater advantages. Inclusion in the Federation would add one to the ten legislatures of Canada and the seven legislatures of Australia. The peoples of those Dominions may perhaps feel that a federation within a federation, for such small populations as they possess, is a complicated extravagance. The increased cost would be, however, far more than offset by the reduction in the cost of defence. The provision of armed forces to defend such large territories containing such small populations is an extremely expensive matter, while their proportion of the cost of the defence of the Federation would be very small. They would gain complete security from external aggression at a small fraction of the present cost. There would also be very substantial economic advantages. They would gain at once "Imperial pre-ference" in the whole of Western Europe and the dependencies of Western Europe. In due course they would obtain a completely free market. While they are protected from European competition by their distance from Europe, they would gain an immense advantage over other extra-European countries because of the ability of their goods to pass under the Western European tariff wall.

It might be necessary, in order to secure agreement, to make special arrangements as to tariffs. It is possible, for instance, that France would require some protection for its agriculture against cheap Canadian wheat; and it is similarly possible that the Dominions would insist on protecting their industries against European competition. Provisions to that end have not been inserted into my draft because I believe that the gains from free trade within the Federation would far more than offset the loss of protection. This is, however, a matter for argument, and one would not be so dogmatic as to exclude the Dominions by a refusal to compromise.

It seems probable in any case that the Dominions would not allow free immigration from Western Europe and would not enter a federation if free migration were a *sine qua non*. There is some ground for saying that their immigration restrictions have been ill-advised, but they have almost unanimous support from public opinion in the Dominions. I have, therefore, inserted a qualification in Article XVIII, section 5.

There is a further difficulty in the case of the Union of South Africa. Unlike the other countries proposed for the Federation it has a large non-European population. Of its total population of 10 millions, only about 2 millions are of European origin. Since its coloured population is, for practical purposes, unrepresented in its own legislature, it could not expect representation in the Federation as a nation of 10 million people. On the other hand, a colour bar of this character is not in accordance with European traditions, though none of

the European nations has yet found possible the grant
of complete self-government to the coloured populations
of its colonial territories. It would certainly give rise
to political controversy in the Federal Legislature. However, no one assumes that there will not be controversy,
and 8 million coloured South Africans are but a drop in
the vast coloured ocean of the British, French and Dutch
colonial territories. The difficulty should be realised,
but it is not important.

The physical detachment of the Dominions, other
than Eire, from Western Europe must in any case make
their position a little peculiar. It has been emphasised
already that, once federation has been achieved, it must
be indissoluble. The same arguments do not apply to
comparatively small extra-European nations, and it is
possible that a right of secession might help to induce the
Dominions to join. Article I of the draft Constitution
therefore distinguishes between Dominions and other
federated States and gives the former a right of secession.

§ 3.   Newfoundland and Southern Rhodesia.

Newfoundland's responsible Government was suspended temporarily in 1934 and replaced by "Commission" or Crown Colony Government. It is possible
that the war will restore the economic prosperity of the
Island and so enable the system of responsible Government to be reinstated. In any case, the present system is
regarded as merely temporary, and we must make provision on the assumption of a restoration of responsible
government. Though it was not a member of the League

of Nations, there is no reason why it should not be admitted to the Federation on the same basis as the other Dominions, if and when responsible Government is restored.

Southern Rhodesia has responsible Government, subject to restrictions, however, in respect of native affairs. Though the white population numbers only 60,000 and the colony has never been a member of the League of Nations or given full representation at Imperial Conferences, it follows a policy of its own in respect of all matters which would be left to a federated State. It seems desirable, therefore, that it should be allowed to become a federated State, particularly because it would deprive the Union of South Africa of the distinction of being the only federated State with a large coloured population—in Southern Rhodesia that population numbers nearly $1\frac{1}{2}$ millions. Article I of the draft provides for the possibility that Southern and Northern Rhodesia may be amalgamated.

§ 4. Dominions outside the Federation.

In case any Dominion chooses not to join the Federation, it is desirable to consider solutions for the difficulties mentioned at the beginning of this chapter.

1. The transfer of the defence power from the United Kingdom to the Federation implies that the latter must undertake the moral obligation of the United Kingdom to defend the Dominions. Provision must in any case be made for existing defence obligations of federated States—for instance, the obligations of the United Kingdom towards Portugal, Egypt and Iraq. Provision to

that end, which includes the obligation of defending the Dominions, is contained in Article XIII, section 4, of the draft.

2. The fact that a Dominion outside the Federation would be a neutral while the United Kingdom, as part of the Federation, was at war, would not be a disadvantage, though it would be a change in the existing status of all Dominions except Eire and the Union of South Africa. If the Dominion wishes to declare war on the enemy of the Federation the King could do so on the advice of the Dominion Government. I have considered the desirability of making the defence obligations of the Federation and the Dominions mutual. At present, however, Eire and South Africa are under no obligation to defend the United Kingdom, and the others are under no obligation to give active support to the United Kingdom. I think, therefore, that it would be wise to insert no such provision.

3. The fact that not all the Dominions have separate nationality legislation, and, above all, the fact that the United Kingdom normally makes no distinction between British subjects, constantly gives rise to difficulties. It is of the essence of federation that there should be a common federal citizenship. In view of the strong national feelings of the separate States, however, I have thought it wise to suggest that federal nationality should be the sum of the nationalities of the federated States. The British subject would not in any case give up his allegiance to the Crown; he would merely acquire a new allegiance in addition to that which he owes at present. In view of strong national sentiments it is preferable that emphasis should be placed for purposes of nationality upon the State rather than upon the Federation, and I have assumed that control over nationality and naturalisation would remain a State function. An Irish citizen would remain an Irish citizen, but he would acquire federal citizenship as well. The Irish Parliament would continue

to determine who were Irish citizens and therefore, *pro tanto*, who were federal citizens. The only qualification required, on this assumption, is that British subjects who were also Dominion citizens should not become federal citizens unless their Dominion became a federated State. It is simple enough to insert such a qualification, as is done in Article IV, section 2: but it is necessary also to meet the case where Dominion law has not defined Dominion citizenship. This is a matter of detail, but I have thought it wise to give to British subjects domiciled in a Dominion outside the Federation the right to "opt" for federal citizenship. The exercise of the option would not deprive them of their British nationality: it would do no more than make them federal citizens as well.

4. Since under my scheme the control of migration is transferred to the Federation after an interval, the free entry of British subjects into the United Kingdom might eventually be restricted. The case for free entry of British subjects is not, however, any stronger than the case for free entry of others. The Dominions impose severe restrictions on the entry of all persons, whether British subjects or not, and I see no reason why there should not be, if thought desirable, the same restriction in the United Kingdom. Moreover, my plan contemplates free migration within Western Europe. Obviously, we could not insist on a gap being made in the immigration control of the Federation by allowing extra-European British subjects to enter Europe through the United Kingdom without control. This argument is all the stronger if the principle which I have embodied in Article XVIII, section 5, is accepted.

5. The effect of Article XVII of the draft would be to extend to the whole of Western Europe the advantages which the United Kingdom and Eire at present grant under the Ottawa Agreements and other arrangements for imperial preference. This is an essential part of the

scheme, since the aim is in due course to create a great free-trade *bloc* in Western Europe, to the great advantage of the people of the Federation. At the end of an interval, whose length need not be particularly specified, tariff control would be vested in the Federation. There is, of course, nothing to prevent the Federation from agreeing with a Dominion for mutual reductions of tariffs. Such reductions would accrue, however, for the benefit of the whole of Western Europe and not solely for the benefit of Eire and the United Kingdom. The solution of this particular difficulty would be the entry of the Dominion into the Federation.

§ 5. India and Burma.

The position of colonies is considered in the next chapter, and for simplicity of drafting the term "dependencies" is given a wide meaning which includes India and Burma. It is desirable to say a few words at this stage about the position of India and Burma because they are represented at Imperial Conferences and India is a member of the League of Nations.

India and Burma together have a population of over 350 millions, of whom over 80 per cent are illiterate, though a minority in each country (and a larger proportion in Burma than in India) have attained Western standards of education. The standard of living, too, is extremely low. It is evident that neither could be brought into the Federation on the same basis as the European nations. Their population is 75 per cent larger than the combined populations of Western Europe and therefore they could, if given vote for vote, swamp the European votes. The greater part of that population, too, has no conception of the European problems which it is the primary object of federation to solve.

Further, the powers which the Federation would exercise are at present controlled by the British Government. To admit India and Burma on the basis of a limited number of nominated members would be to give the United Kingdom additional votes. On the other hand, they will attain self-government in due course, and it is possible that this stage will be reached during the present war or a short time after its termination. It is obvious that at some time they must, if they so wish, be admitted to the Federation. It is equally obvious that they could not, without upsetting the balance of the Constitution, be brought in on the basis of vote for vote. The solution to this problem seems to be to give India and Burma, when fully self-governing, representation in the Federal Legislature in rough proportion to their interest in European affairs. Representatives could be elected by proportional representation by their legislatures. I should be inclined to equate India with Canada and Burma with New Zealand for purposes of representation.

This is not, however, a problem which need be faced at the moment, and I have included no special provision in the Constitution. India and Burma could be admitted as new States under section 6 of Article I "on such conditions as may be prescribed".

CHAPTER IV

COLONIES

§ 1. The Return of German Colonies.

It happens that at no time during the past century has one nation of Western Europe declared war on another nation of Western Europe because of its colonial claims. In the late nineteenth century, however, war was avoided on several occasions only by a hair's breadth. Great Britain and France might easily have fought over Egypt, the Sudan, or the Niger. Great Britain and Russia touched the verge of battle through the Russian approach to Afghanistan and had conflicts over what is now Iran. Great Britain and Germany had numerous disputes over West Africa, the Transvaal, New Guinea and Samoa. France and Germany nearly fought over Morocco. There were difficulties, too, in China and Tangier. Even the United States and Great Britain had boundary disputes in North America and in relation to British Guiana. Colonial wars actually broke out between the United States and Spain and between Italy and Turkey.

Boundaries are now reasonably well delineated, and there are few portions of the earth's surface now available for colonial occupation without challenging some existing power. It is just that fact that gives the present situation one of its most dangerous elements. If a nation like

Germany or Italy considers that for reasons of prestige or economics it wants *Lebensraum*, there is no means by which this aim may be achieved except the invasion of a small nation or the picking of a quarrel with a great power. Armed forces are built up on each side in order to strengthen the demand on the one side and the refusal on the other. The German Navy, in particular, was developed for the avowed purpose of supporting German demands for colonial territories. War did not break out in 1911 because the German Navy was not ready. It broke out in 1914 over a different issue when the Navy still was not strong enough. No one in Britain doubts that, if Hitler had satiated his appetite for European territory, he would have built a navy to support his demand for colonies. No one ought to doubt that, if Germany is allowed to revive at the end of the present war, one of the first steps in the revival will be the building of naval and aerial forces.

A federation in which Germany is included would prevent any such occurrence. It would also be fully strong enough to defend the colonies of its members against aggression by other nations. It would not, however, have solved the colonial problem by reason of that fact alone. Germany and Italy were late in attaining national unity and therefore were late in the scramble for colonies. Germany obtained some territories, but lost them in 1918. Italy has had to pick quarrels in North Africa and to absorb another European nation without entirely satisfying its appetite. For reasons explained in Chapter II, Italy cannot at present be included in a federation, and would be compelled either to make arrangements with the Federation (for instance, by accepting the Federal Constitution for limited purposes under Article I, section 7), or risk a war with the Federation by attacking some State outside the Federation.

The problem of satisfying German colonial ambitions, within the framework of the Federation, remains. The possibility of securing the return to Germany of the colonies transferred to the Allied and Associated Powers in 1919, and now under the mandate of the League of Nations, seems to me to be remote. These mandated territories have been administered as an integral part of British, French, Belgian, Australian, South African and New Zealand territory for more than twenty years. Money has been spent on their development, citizens of those States have acquired rights there, and generally there is a body of vested interests which would have considerable propaganda power. It seems to be the firm opinion of colonial experts, too, not based on political prejudice, that the methods of colonial administration adopted by Germany did not accord with principles of trusteeship. I personally base no substantial argument on this assertion. Whatever ⸱solution of the colonial problem be found, there must clearly be an element of federal control which would prevent, for instance, the exploitation of natural resources and native labour for the benefit of the colonial power. Moreover, we are not entitled to assume that the methods adopted by the slave-drivers of the German Empire or the Nazi Reich will necessarily be adopted by a democratic Germany. The argument is worth mentioning, however, because it adds somewhat to the psychological argument which seems to me to be fundamental.

The assumption on which we are proceeding is that Germany will be defeated in the present war—in the sense, at least, that the present regime will disappear and a democratic Government ready to agree to reasonable terms of peace will be established. If this does not happen, most of the argument in this book becomes irrelevant, and other possibilities need not be considered. The plan considered in this book is put forth because I believe that it provides a just and workable alternative to the only other solution, which is the dismemberment of Germany. It assumes that public opinion will be enlightened enough to offer full and equal collaboration to a democratic Germany. I find it difficult to believe, however, that opinion will be so enlightened as to allow the actual restoration of colonial territory to Germany as a reward for the support which most Germans have given to Nazi aggression in Eastern Europe. I feel certain that South Africa, Australia and New Zealand would not give up their mandated territories. One could hardly ask Belgium to give up such territories; and I have doubts about British opinion and even more about French opinion.

I suggest the return of the mandated territories to Germany, then, as a possibility, though a very remote possibility. There is, of course, an alternative which seemed attractive to me when I first considered these problems. It is the transfer to the Federation of all colonial territories.

§ 2. Transfer to the Federation.

The attractiveness of this proposal as a practical proposition disappeared when its implications were examined. It has the enormous advantage of solving the whole colonial problem by a surgical operation. It is essentially just because it would provide for absolute equality. It would, I think, be easier to persuade British opinion, at least, to make a grand sacrifice in the general interests of European peace (though I have no illusions about the extent of the opposition) than it would be to persuade that opinion to make particular sacrifices to Germany. I feel sure, nevertheless, that it is not a practical proposition.

We have attempted, and with a fair measure of success, to create among our colonial peoples a loyalty to the Crown. The French have been perhaps even more successful in converting their colonial peoples into French citizens. The proposition involves that we now ask them to transfer their loyalty to a new organisation. Large numbers of European colonists have settled in the territories and must, if the proposal is carried out, for effective purposes lose their nationality. Vested interests are likely to feel that they would suffer—though I believe that they would gain—from federal control. Nations, and especially the British nations, have been taught to regard with pride the extent of their colonial possessions, even if they have also been taught—as, quite often, they have not—that colonies create responsibilities and obligations rather than assets. These seem to me to be formidable obstacles to transfer.

The extent of the obstacles did not in itself seem to me to be entirely convincing, but I could find no very good answers to a number of very practical questions that the proposition compels one to ask. Are the inhabitants, or the inhabitants other than Europeans, to lose their existing nationality? What is to be the official language of administration?—a question far more important in a colony than in Europe. How is the civil service to be recruited? Will the discussion of colonial matters in the Federal Legislature prevent effective discussion of the essential European questions? Will colonial issues cause difficulties in federal elections? Will the colonial representatives disappear from the French Parliament? These and other questions can be answered, but the cumulative difficulties, added to the initial difficulties of persuasion, reach substantial proportion. I have therefore come to the conclusion that if we proposed that colonies should be transferred to the Federation we are more likely to prevent federation than to assist it. While the proposal might render the federal idea more attractive to some nations, it might prevent the support of federation by the United Kingdom and France, without whose support, in fact, the whole federal idea is futile.

The rejection of the principle of transferring all colonies to the Federation does not assume that no colonies will be transferred. Nationalistic propaganda has done much to persuade public opinion that colonies are assets, no matter how impoverished they may be, and no matter how great the cost of administration. Such propaganda has naturally resulted in competition from other powers for territories which intelligent people would not acquire except as a public duty. If the obligations suggested later in this chapter are accepted, the burden of colonial liabilities will become more apparent and, as imperialist ideas die down, it may be much easier for States to agree to transfer territories to the Federation. Such territories would probably consist in the main of poor areas where white settlement was difficult or not worth while, and where the native tribes were in a very primitive condition—in Central Africa, for instance—and in such cases the difficulty of practical administration would not be great. I have therefore inserted a provision in Article XVI, section 3, to meet this possibility of transfer.

§ 3. Colonial Limitations.

Colonies not transferred to the Federation must come under a limited federal control so as to provide equality for all federal citizens in the advantages and responsibilities of colonial government. If, as is proposed, the Federation becomes a free-trade area, the colonies will become part of that area and the application of mercantilist theories by any State will become impossible. On the other hand, it seems extremely unlikely that States would accept free migration between Europe and the colonies. Under the scheme which I have embodied

in the draft Constitution the Federation would control
migration so far as Europe was concerned, whereas the
colonial power would have the power so far as its colonies
were concerned, though laws made by the federated
State for a colony could be disallowed by the Federation.
Immigration into colonies is largely a matter of what
the Americans call "police power", that is, of the internal
regulation of the order and health of the colony. On the
other hand, the Federation must be able in any event to
prevent discrimination between citizens of the colonial
power and other federal citizens. Whether this is enough
is a matter for argument, and I should not regard the
change as fundamental if control over migration were
vested in the Federation. In that case, some provision
would have to be made for the dependencies of the
Dominions. For reasons given in the previous chapter,
the draft permits the Dominions to regulate migration
in respect of their own territories. It would be extremely
difficult to operate a system in which, for example, the
Union of South Africa controlled immigration into the
Union while the Federation controlled immigration into
South-West Africa.

These restrictions follow from the general arrangements contemplated for the exercise of federal powers.
They are not adequate in themselves as a substitute for
the alternative proposal of transferring colonies to the
Federation. There should be additional restrictions going
somewhat further than those imposed on mandatories
under Article 22 of the Covenant of the League of
Nations.

1. The general principle of "trusteeship" for the native races which is embodied in the Covenant should clearly be generalised. Though German and Italian statesmen apparently assume that colonies are and ought to be maintained for the advantage of the colonial power, the more enlightened opinion elsewhere insists that authority over colonies is an obligation and not in itself a benefit. The generalisation of the principle of trusteeship would accord with the recent policy of the Colonial Office, though there have been occasions when pressure from the European population of the colonies has caused that policy to waver; and it is by no means agreed that the Ottawa Agreements were for the benefit of the indigenous inhabitants.

2. Even though the principle of trusteeship is applied, it is hardly practicable to assume that the colonies should be "reserves" for the indigenous races; nor, indeed, would the conditions of these races be improved by the withdrawal of European capital and enterprise. On the other hand, the German case is not met if the citizens of the colonial power derive peculiar advantages from their colonies. The colonial power should be, in a sense, trustee for the world as well as trustee for the native races. Accordingly, the colonies should be open to the capital and enterprise of all federal citizens without discrimination in favour of the citizens of the colonial power. Naturally, the official language of administration would continue to be that of the colonial power, and the prescription of that language could not be regarded as a discrimination in favour of the citizens of the colonial power, though it would have that effect.

3. It is part of the German case that while the trained citizens of a colonial power have careers open to them in the colonial administration and judicial services, the trained citizens of Germany have no such opportunity. It is, I think, reasonable to suggest that the colonial

services should be open to all federal citizens. The opportunities would not be equal, since language tests would impose a disqualification. If a Frenchman, a Netherlander or a German is prepared to become English-speaking for official purposes, there is no reason why he should not be admitted to the British colonial service.

4. The welfare of the colonies would be a concern of the Federation. It should have official knowledge of developments in colonial policy, of changes in economic conditions, and of difficulties in administration. This is important not only because the Federation must provide means for securing that the restrictions are properly observed, but also because it may be called upon, under its defence power, to defend a colony against external aggression and to assist the colonial power in putting down internal disorder.

It is obvious that there must be a means for securing the observance of these restrictions. It is equally obvious that they cannot be left to decisions of the courts. To ask the courts to determine whether a colonial law was "for the well-being and development of the people of the colony" would be to ask them to investigate questions on which the judges were entirely ignorant. The means for keeping federated States within their legal powers under the Federal Constitution are considered in a later chapter. It will be seen that the practice of "disallowance" of State legislation, which is capable of being applied generally in Canada, is recommended for adoption in respect of a number of restrictions in State activity. The effect of disallowance is to enable the political organs of the Federation to declare State legislation to be invalid. Instead of leaving the courts to decide whether the legislation is valid or not, the appropriate political organ decides, within the limits of the Constitution, whether it is desirable or not. Whatever be the merits or demerits of this system as applied generally—a question which we need not argue at this stage—it seems clear that for present purposes judicial review is not appropriate and that disallowance is a better method. Provision to that effect is contained in Article XVI, section 6, of the draft.

§ 4. A Colonial Commission.

The disallowance of colonial legislation would not be the only colonial function of the Federation. It would also be charged with the defence of colonies—the question whether the colonial power should also keep a colonial force is discussed below (and see Article XVI, section 8, of the draft). Also, it might be desirable to permit the use of federal funds, with the consent of the colonial power, for the purpose of colonial development. If the principle of trusteeship is accepted and insisted upon, and if few special advantages from colonial development accrue directly to the colonial power, there will always be a temptation, especially in times of economic stress, to economise at the expense of the colonies. In Great Britain, for instance, a Treasury with its eyes on the next budget has at times been very reluctant to provide funds for economic development in the colonies or for the provision of educational facilities. This tendency has not been restricted to "Little England" Governments. Mr Joseph Chamberlain, for instance, complained of the niggardliness of Sir Michael Hicks-Beach. The Federation will have a wide field for its revenues and, in view of the variety of its various territories, it is likely to be hit by industrial depression less hardly than any of the federated States standing alone. Moreover, the Federation would be in a position to suggest joint action by colonial powers—for instance, by the United Kingdom, France and Belgium in Central Africa. Grants would of course be given only on specified conditions, and the Federation would need to provide machinery for determining the nature of those conditions and the results of its assistance.

Questions of this character could be left to the ordinary political machinery of the Federation. British experience suggests, however, that colonial administration on the basis of fixed principles is rather a question of administration than a question of policy. Parliament is unable to devote enough time to colonial questions, and such questions rarely raise issues for party debate. The Colonial Office is apt to go its own way without substantial changes in its routine. Except where colonies were actually transferred to it the Federation would not have administrative functions, but would be concerned with a limited range of powers which need not, we hope, often raise issues for debate in the Federal Legislature. The ordinary process of government therefore seems hardly appropriate. On the contrary, the functions imply only a development of the functions of the Mandates Commission of the League of Nations, a body which has done extremely well with its very limited powers.

My draft (Article XVI, sections 1 and 2) therefore contains provision for the establishment of a Colonial Commission. It would exercise functions conferred upon it by federal legislation as well as functions conferred directly by the Constitution. If colonies were transferred to the Federation, for instance, federal legislation might give additional powers to the Commission. I have not specifically provided that such colonies should be controlled by the Commission. That might be a convenient method. On the other hand it might not, because colonial administration does sometimes raise political questions for which the Federal Government would have to take responsibility. Moreover, I contemplate, for reasons given below, that the Commission would be composed of expert critics rather than of expert administrators or of politicians. It is a wise precaution not to insert in a constitution anything that can be left to legislation, since legislation is more easily altered than a constitution.

The functions which are set out in the Constitution are as follows:

1. The power of disallowance could not be exercised without a resolution of the Commission (except for laws in force at the establishment of the Federation). This gives a reasonable safeguard against abuse of the right of disallowance, provided that the Commission is a reasonably impartial and "non-political" body.

2. Grants could be made for colonial development only on the recommendation of the Commission. If the Commission were a reasonably impartial and "non-political" body, such grants would then not be made for "log-rolling" or purely party purposes.

3. A colonial defence force could be maintained by the colonial power only if the Commission so recommended. Given the assumption on which we are working, that armed forces in general would be vested in the Federation, and that the States would have none, it will be understood that the maintenance of a colonial defence force would be dangerous. An Indian Army, for instance, might become an instrument of aggression against the Federation or some other federated State. On the other hand, it might be more convenient for the Federation to allow the creation of small colonial forces, subject to rigid restrictions, which would depend on the nature and conditions of the colony. For instance, a small army might be required to maintain order in Palestine or to protect the North-West Frontier in India. While permission to maintain such a force would be a political issue to be decided by the Federal Government and Legislature, expert knowledge of the colonial circumstances would be required. Further, if the Federation could not act without the recommendation of an expert and impartial Commission, other powers could reasonably assume that permission to enrol an armed force would not be granted to a colonial power by a reckless majority for doubtful political reasons.

4. It is a necessary consequence of federation that the Federation should guarantee the maintenance of order in colonies as well as in Europe. Indeed, the problem of maintaining order is much more acute in a colony where racial and religious disputes sometimes occur. One could not justify the use of federal forces to bolster mal-administration by the colonial power. On the other hand, the armed support must be given immediately, and without examination of causes and effects, lest serious injury be caused to life and property. The Federation might thus be placed in the dilemma of being compelled to assist the colonial power in enforcing a policy which the colonial power ought never to have adopted. In some

degree, the power of disallowance meets this difficulty. It should, however, be plain to a colonial power that it could not use the federal force to carry out a futile and dangerous policy. Accordingly, though one could not suggest that federal force should not be used without the consent of the Commission, I think it necessary that the Commission should have powers to recommend the withdrawal of assistance (Article XVI, section 9). This is a "big stick" or sanctioning power which would probably not be used: but British experience has shown that the existence of such powers (as in central control of local government) enables representations against policy to be made more emphatically and more effectively. It would enable the Commission to say: "We think this policy is likely to lead to disaster; we recommend you to change it; and we warn you that if it led to disaster we might have to recommend that no assistance be given to you towards putting down the disorder."

5. Finally, the annual colonial reports would be submitted to the Commission so that it could undertake the same survey of colonial conditions as the Mandates Commission now makes for the League of Nations. This alone is a function of considerable importance, because it would compel the colonial power to disclose information and justify its administration.

It will be seen, then, that the Commission should be expert and not political, that its functions would occupy the whole time of its members, and that it should be reasonably independent. In the provision that I have drafted (Article XVI, section 2) I have not prescribed their qualifications, believing that it is safe to leave such prescription to the Federal Legislature. In any case, qualifications of this character can easily be largely fictitious we have had experience in Britain and in South Africa—

and it is undesirable that the Commission should be held up by legal proceedings challenging the validity of appointments, as would be necessary if a provision relating to qualifications were inserted. I have, however, insisted that members of the Legislature, or persons holding offices of profit in the Federation or in any federated State, should not be appointed. Membership of the Commission should be a full-time occupation, and in any case I am anxious to keep out, as far as is practicable, the party element. The technical phrase "office of profit" is used because honorary offices, including membership of the House of Lords, ought not to disqualify.

I have also provided a six-year term. This is longer by one year than the maximum duration of the Federal Legislature, and on occasion new appointments might have to be made by the Legislature at the end of its life. This difficulty cannot be overcome unless we permit a new Parliament to elect a new Commission, in which case the party element would almost certainly enter. I have made reappointment possible, and I hope that the tradition would be established. I have also allowed removal, though this would require the consent of both Houses as well as the consent of the Federal Government. To strengthen the comparatively secure tenure which these provisions give, I have provided also that the salary of a member shall not be reduced during his term of office. Constitutional practice is always more important than the written word, but I believe that these provisions give a reasonable prospect of forming a Colonial Commission of the kind required.

CHAPTER V

FEDERAL GOVERNMENT

§ 1. Presidential or Parliamentary?

The question of colonies has been examined before the question of federal organisation for two reasons. In the first place, it is desirable to understand the nature and size of the territories over which the federal authorities will operate before consideration is given to the nature of those authorities. In the second place, this book is addressed primarily to British readers, and among the first questions which they will ask will be: "Does this mean the disruption of the British Empire?" The answer has been given in many pages, but it can be expressed in a word of one syllable: No. We hope that the Dominions will join with the United Kingdom: but whether they do or do not their relations to the Crown will not in substance be altered. The Colonies and other dependencies will remain British, but we shall share the advantages, if any, and, I hope, the burdens, too, with others, as we have always asserted that we are willing to do. In addition, we shall share the advantages and the burdens of the French and Dutch dependencies.

When we turn to questions of a purely constitutional order, previous discussions enable us to answer one question out of hand. The Federation is to be a democratic federation, and must therefore have at least one House of the Legislature elected by the people. The initial problem not yet discussed involves consideration of the relations between that House and the Federal Government. There are three kinds of precedents, the system adopted in Switzerland, which is commonly known as "directorial"; the system operated in the United States and some South American countries, which may be called "presidential"; and the system of responsible government based upon British practice and in force in most democratic countries, including the federations of Canada and Australia.

The Swiss system implies responsibility to the Legislature in the sense that the Federal Council, or Government, is elected by the National Council, or lower House, and that it is dependent on it for finance and legislative powers. Its seven members are, however, not members of either House of the Legislature, and they have a fixed term of office—four years like the members of the National Council themselves. They cannot be dismissed, nor can they dissolve the National Council. In theory, this system should lead to constant deadlocks between the two Councils. If we tried to adopt it in Great Britain, after our long experience of a different kind, we should probably have such deadlocks. If a nation less accustomed to political compromises than the Swiss and the British were to adopt it, there would probably be permanent deadlock. In practice in Switzerland no difficulty arises. The Federal Council bows to the national will as represented by the National Council. If a proposal is defeated, another is made. If the National Council will not authorise a particular item of expenditure, then the money cannot be spent. The Federal Council is not a party body; its members are commonly drawn from several parties. Moreover, members are generally re-elected for as long as they are willing and able to act. In 1935, for instance, two members had been in office since 1912; five spoke German, one French and one Italian; five were Catholics and two Protestants; one belonged to the Catholic Conservative Party and six to the Radical Party. Since 1935 there has been one change only. From 1848 to 1929 members had an average period of office of eleven years. During that time, only one Councillor failed to secure re-election when he was a candidate.

This remarkable stability is due to factors which cannot, I think, be copied. The practice continues an old cantonal tradition which, unlike some "traditions", is not easily created. The political problems of Switzerland have rarely been difficult of solution. In spite of their differences in language and religion, the Swiss have achieved a remarkable national unity. Like the British, they have learned to compromise. Finally, party organisation in the British or the American sense has hardly developed, and for a period of 46 years after the constitutional reform of 1874, the Radical Party possessed a majority in the National Council. It has had no majority since 1919, but it has held the largest number of seats and has been able to secure the collaboration of other parties.

This remarkable combination of factors could never be copied in a European federation. The directorial system would make for deadlock and would therefore result in weak government or, what is worse, no government at all. Weakness in government, indeed, commonly leads to the other extreme, a coup d'état establishing a dictatorial regime. If this is so, we cannot suggest the adoption of the Swiss form of government.

In the American system, the ordinary powers of administration are vested in the President, who in substance derives his authority, under the Constitution, from his election by the people of the United States. He holds office for a fixed term of four years, but may be re-elected. He cannot be removed from office except on impeachment by the House of Representatives, tried by the Senate. Neither the President nor any of the members of his Cabinet sits in either House of Congress. His salary is determined by Congress, but may not be increased or diminished during his term of office. His position under the Constitution is therefore independent of the legislature, except in respect of impeachment. On the other hand, he has no independent legislative power, and though he can veto Congressional legislation, that veto can be overridden by a vote of two-thirds of the members present in each House. The expenses of government are voted by Congress and he has no governmental revenues without such a vote. He has power to make treaties, but only with the concurrence of two-thirds of the Senate. The concurrence of the Senate is also required for the appointment by him of ambassadors,

other public ministers and consuls, judges of the Supreme
Court, and many other officers. Only Congress can
declare war. He has certain other powers of less importance which do not require express Congressional
sanction, though of course Congressional authority is
required for any expenditure which they involve.

The President is thus both independent and dependent. The difficulties inherent in this system of "checks
and balances" have been offset by the two-party system.
If his party has a majority in both Houses—as President
Franklin Roosevelt has, for instance—he can often secure
the concurrence of Congress by arrangement with the
Party leaders in each House. Party divisions are not,
however, so strict as they are in the British Parliament,
and cross-voting is not only frequent but usual. Technically, he has no power to introduce legislation into
Congress, though he can inform Congress by message
of his opinion that legislation is necessary. He can then
use backstairs methods to secure the introduction of such
legislation by a member. Even so he may be defeated,
as President Roosevelt has often been. In order to keep
a majority, the use of "patronage" to persuade members
is almost essential, though it has never been corrupt
patronage of the kind familiar in eighteenth-century
England because Congressmen may not hold other offices
under the United States.

It often happens, however, that the President and
one or both of the Houses of Congress are drawn from
different parties and are, in fact, in strong opposition.
The possibilities of deadlock are thus substantial. They

are offset by the fact that Congress can impose duties upon the President, though it cannot compel him to exercise them eagerly. In practice, too, neither President nor Congress has carried opposition to extremes. Congress does not fail to vote supplies merely because it dislikes the President's politics, though it does vote supplies more readily for policies approved by Congress and determines how much shall be spent on each service.

Moreover, the independence of the President means also the independence of Congress. In the United Kingdom special groups of interests like the trade unions, the mineowners, the farmers, and so on, must persuade the Government if they wish special advantages. The Government considers the policy of the country as a whole, with reference to their future political support. A Congressman, on the other hand, is concerned only with his electoral support in his own riding or constituency, and the task of any such interest is to persuade a majority of Congressmen. Hence many of the peculiarities of American politics. Congressmen are "lobbied" by "pressure groups" to persuade them to support particular policies. Deals are effected by groups of Congressmen often under the stimulus of professional lobbyists; thereby the principle of "you scratch my back and I'll scratch yours" is carried out. Strongly organised bodies, like the Veterans of the Great War, can secure a "distribution of the pork barrel" to the enrichment of their members. Those who established the Constitution of the United States deduced from the

corruption of Parliament by George III and his ministers—a corruption which did so much to cause the
American Revolution—that Congress should be independent of the executive. At the same time, they were
not anxious to make the President too dependent on
Congress, because they feared "democracy" as much
as Whigs and Tories alike in England. Nor could they
make the President too independent because they would
be accused (as, indeed, they were) of trying to restore
"monarchy"—as much a term of abuse as "democracy".
The result was a series of compromises which has worked
only because the Americans have never forgotten how
to compromise.

It is not my purpose, nor indeed am I qualified, to
criticise the Constitution of the United States. American
authorities no longer regard it as the acme of wisdom.
Nor is it possible to elaborate any constitution by a series
of compromises which shall not have almost as many
defects as it has advantages. The circumstances which
caused these compromises are not the circumstances
which we have to consider. A constitution should be as
simple as the conditions of the time permit, and there
is nothing simpler than the essential principle of responsible government. This does not mean that the British
system is simple: one who has written over a thousand
pages in describing how part of it works[1] could not dare
to make such an assertion. What is suggested is that
the essential principle is simple and forms a basis on

[1] *Cabinet Government* (1936) and *Parliament* (1939).

which a working constitution can be erected by a slow growth of practice.

The task of the draftsman is not to provide a constitution in any true sense, but only to provide its framework. Provided that the essential factors are included, the less rigid the outline the better. Experience, not draftsmen, produces constitutions. France and Great Britain have built different structures on the same foundation, and we have no reason to believe that a Federation of Western Europe could not do the same. We can feel reasonably certain that the constitutional systems of Switzerland and the United States would not work in Europe. We cannot hope that the Federal Legislature will be for some time to come a body of federal representatives; they will be German, French, British, Norwegian, and the rest, until the federal tradition has been established. Still less can we believe that an elected President would be or could be the focus of a European allegiance. It would not be impossible to work the American system. No constitution will work unless the people concerned want it to work: if they want it to work they can work any system. We could, no doubt, secure the election as President of some benevolent and able neutral citizen to cover the initial establishment. Our legislators would realise that they had to work with him and enable him to govern. If the choice lay between the Constitution of the United States or no federation I would unhesitatingly advocate the former.

That, however, is not the choice. The simpler and the more easily intelligible the constitution the easier it will work. Responsible government is not only simpler but it is understood by all Western Europeans. It is in operation in all the countries suggested for inclusion except Germany and Switzerland, and Germany had a form of responsible government between 1919 and 1933. These systems differ widely among themselves, and the federal system would differ from them all. Such a result is inevitable because each political unit develops its institutions in accordance with its own experience. Our task is only to establish a body of principles which avoids friction and enables experience to operate. I assume, therefore, that responsible government would be the principle of the Federation.

§ 2. The People's House.

It is essential to any true federal system that it should possess a legislature in which at least one House is directly elected by the people of the Federation. I have called it the "People's House" because that term enables one to distinguish it from the lower Houses in the federated States. It is also the invariable practice that the peoples of the several States should be represented in it roughly according to population. This is done because it is the only fair method of representation which can be reached without interminable haggling over numbers. It gives, of course, a preponderance to the larger States, and it was for this reason that in the United States—and the example has been followed by Australia and Switzerland—another House was created with *equal* representation of States. Proposals are elaborated below for off-setting the dominance of Germany, the United Kingdom, and France by setting up a second Chamber.

If we assume one representative for each complete million inhabitants, with one representative in addition for a fraction of a million greater than a half, we reach the following composition:

People's House

	Popula-tion	Repre-sentation
Australia	6·62	7
Belgium	8·25	8
Canada	10·38	10
Denmark (with dependen-cies in Europe)	3·61	4
Eire	3·00	3
Finland	3·67	4
France	42·00	42
Germany (with the Saar, Austria and Sudetenland)	76·64	77
United Kingdom	47·57	48
Iceland	·12	—
Luxemburg	·30	—
Netherlands	8·56	9
Newfoundland	·29	—
New Zealand	1·63	2
Norway	3·00	3
South Africa (European population only)	2·00	2
Southern Rhodesia (Euro-pean population only)	·06	—
Sweden	6·21	6
Switzerland	4·10	4
	228·01	229

It is proposed below, however, that, as in the case of Canada, no State should have a lower representation in the lower Chamber than it has in the upper Chamber. Assuming the distribution provided by Article X of the draft, the representation would be changed to the following:

	Proportional representation	Actual representation
Australia	7	7
Belgium	8	8
Canada	10	10
Denmark	4	5
Eire	3	5
Finland	4	5
France	42	42
Germany	77	77
United Kingdom	48	48
Iceland	—	3
Luxemburg	—	3
Netherlands	9	9
Newfoundland	—	3
New Zealand	2	5
Norway	3	5
South Africa	2	5
Southern Rhodesia	—	3
Sweden	6	6
Switzerland	4	5

The change would have the advantage of increasing the representation of the smaller powers from 27 per cent to almost one-third, though it is, I think, extremely unlikely that the representatives of the three great powers would be unanimous in opposition to a unanimous representation from the smaller States. The representation of the British Commonwealth (including Eire) would be increased from 31 to 35 per cent, while the German representation would be decreased from just over one-third to 31 per cent.

It is questionable, however, whether the population of a federated State is the right criterion. It will have been observed that in the above list only the European population of the Union of South Africa and of Southern Rhodesia was taken into consideration. This was done not because it was thought that any "colour bar" was desirable, but because a federated State can hardly claim to count for purposes of federal representation a section of the population that it does not count for representation in its own political institutions. In the United States the untaxed Indians were not counted, while the slaves were counted as three-fifths. This latter arrangement was a compromise directed to prevent the Southern States from being over-weighted by the Northern States, and is not in point here. In Australia it was provided that "if by the law of any State all persons of any race are disqualified from voting for the more numerous House of the Parliament of the State, then in reckoning the number of the people of the State or of the Commonwealth, persons of that race resident in that State shall not be counted".

If it were only a question of South Africa and Rhodesia, such a provision might be inserted in the Federal Constitution. We must make the draft, however, on the assumption that other States might be admitted at some future time, and the question would then arise whether a democracy with a restricted franchise should be represented for federal purposes according to its population. I think primarily of the position of India, which would, I hope, be admitted at an early stage. The population of India and Burma in 1931 was over 350 millions, so that on the basis of representation by population India and Burma together could outvote all the other federated States. Democratic representation, however, is at present provided only in the Provinces of British India (and in Burma), where 30 million people have the franchise.

This case is extreme, though similar considerations might, at a later stage in the world's history, apply to Japan and China. It may reasonably be urged that these are problems which can be left for settlement until they arise. It might save future difficulty, however, if we could meet the problem now. Moreover, it may not be a problem limited to Asia. If a State of Eastern Europe, with a limited franchise, were admitted to the Federation, it seems reasonable to assume that its representation would be according to its franchise rather than according to its population.

My draft Constitution therefore begins from a different angle. It assumes (Article IX) one member for every 500,000 *federal electors*. It leaves to the Federal Legislature the task of defining who are federal electors, but, until the Federal Legislature exercises that power, they will be the persons who have the franchise for State elections. This does not solve the problem, for it gives

India a representation of sixty and the United Kingdom a representation of about sixty-two. Moreover, it would raise difficulties in such countries as France, where only males have the franchise. The alternatives both have advantages and disadvantages but, the second being slightly the more complicated, I put it forward for discussion.

The electoral areas and the method of election must ultimately be determined by the Federal Legislature. It is necessary to make some provision, however, to cover the period which must elapse before laws on this subject can be made. The case for single-member constituencies is obviously much less strong in respect of the federal system than it is in the internal constitutional system of a State. Assuming one representative for every million inhabitants, the County of London would be divided into four constituencies, Lancashire into five, Middlesex into four, and the West Riding of Yorkshire into three. Alternatively, the towns might be separately represented, in which case Birmingham would have one representative and other towns would be grouped. Leeds, Bradford and Hull, for instance, would have one member.

It is questionable, however, whether local interests need be represented in this way. So far as foreign affairs, defence and colonies are concerned, there is no need to distinguish Lancashire from Yorkshire. Nor is it necessary that for economic purposes one part of Lancashire should be differentiated from another, or one part of London from another. What is more, the Federation will require representatives of national reputation, not local councillors. The party organisation of Great Britain has fortunately prevented the sending to Westminster of too many "favourite sons", but we cannot feel that the same result would be achieved by other countries. We might even contemplate the election of, say, a German as a representative from the British people.

Expressed in British terms, the alternatives are:

(1) Single-member constituencies;
(2) Constituencies formed by geographical counties or groups of counties;
(3) Constituencies formed on the one hand by administrative counties or groups of such counties, and on the other hand by groups of towns;
(4) England, Wales, Scotland and Ireland as constituencies (the Islands being attached to England);
(5) The United Kingdom as a single constituency.

Of these, the fourth seems to me to give adequate representation to such local differences as are of federal importance: and if such a method were adopted in other countries, minorities would secure representation in the People's House. At the same time, the Federation could not in the first instance compel the division of a State in this way, and it seems to be far simpler to treat a State as a single constituency, allowing the State, with the consent of the Federal Government, to make smaller constituencies of itself if it thought fit.

This method would imply proportional representation. If there were a Conservative majority in the United Kingdom or in England, with substantial Labour and

Liberal minorities, the effect of the British system of voting would be totally to deprive the Labour and Liberal parties of representation. In the United Kingdom in 1935 (omitting uncontested seats) the National Government gained only about 1,600,000 votes more than the Opposition parties, in a total poll of 29 millions Yet if the United Kingdom formed one constituency, this 1,600,000 majority would be enough totally to deprive of representation the 10 million electors who voted for the Opposition. On the other hand, if England, Wales, Scotland and Ireland were separate constituencies, England, Scotland and Northern Ireland would have sent Conservatives only, whereas Wales would have sent Labour members only.

Proportional representation has disadvantages—which are so great, for instance, that I would not recommend its adoption for British elections. In particular, it tends towards the creation of small parties powerful only because of their nuisance value, and having little of the sense of responsibility which is to be found among parties where the two-party system operates. If there were any real chance of getting a two-party system in the Federation, I would recommend single-member constituencies with straight voting. I fear, however, that there is no such possibility, and that all Federal Governments would be coalitions. In that event, national constituencies—or regional constituencies—with proportional representation are preferred, as giving a fairer representation of actual political opinion.

§ 3. The States' House.

The problem of a second Chamber is always open for discussion. The case usually made for it is that it imposes a check upon the action of a majority which may have been obtained in the lower House through the accidental conditions of a general election held, perhaps, some years before. It is an argument used by persons of conservative temperament who distrust democratic election, or who consider that restrictions on legislative power are desirable to prevent "extreme" or "wild" or "extravagant" reforms. The result is that most second Chambers are conservative bodies which hinder "radical" legislation but do not obstruct "reactionary" legislation. Consequently, Conservatives think a second Chamber essential and Radicals view any such proposal with suspicion—and the debate continues.

In a federation, however, the problem is simpler. The major consideration in such a system is not reform and obstruction to reform, but the securing of the adhesion of the States to be federated and of their willingness to take part in the operation of the federal machine. If we allow representation according to population in the lower House, we give preponderance to the States with large populations—in our present example, Germany, the United Kingdom, and France. Historical experience does not in fact suggest that the division of opinion is ever between large States and small States. Nevertheless, small States are as patriotic and as sensible of their own importance as the large States, and they are not likely to be content with nothing more than a small fraction of the total representation.

If the People's House were formed strictly according to population, Germany and France, or Germany and the United Kingdom, or France and the British Commonwealth, would have a majority. I do not think that any such combination is possible, because the national representation would certainly be split up between parties, and we should not find the representatives of any great power acting as a solid *bloc*. Nevertheless, the possibility of its happening may be enough to make the entry of small powers difficult.

This problem was overcome in the United States, Switzerland, and Australia, by allowing representation by population in the lower House and equal State representation in the upper House. A combination of small States can then obstruct in the upper House legislation which is forced upon the lower House by a combination of large States—though in point of fact this has never happened, I believe, in any of the three federations. In Canada, this system is modified by giving equal representation not to the provinces but to groups of Provinces. There, Ontario and Quebec have twenty-four senators each. The Maritime Provinces have twenty-four senators divided among the three Provinces so that Nova Scotia and New Brunswick have ten each and Prince Edward Island has four senators. The Western Provinces similarly have twenty-four senators, namely, six for each Province.

But for the proposal to include very small States like Iceland, Luxemburg, Newfoundland, and Southern

Rhodesia, with a total population of little more than
$\frac{3}{4}$ million, I should be content to suggest equal representation. It would be ridiculous, however, to allow
Germany and Southern Rhodesia equal representation.
Accordingly, grading seems to be desirable, so long as
such grading continues to give a superiority to small
States. In Article X of the draft I have suggested the
following allocation:

States' House

Germany	9	New Zealand	5
France	7	Norway	5
United Kingdom	7	South Africa	5
Australia	5	Sweden	5
Belgium	5	Switzerland	5
Canada	5	Iceland	3
Denmark	5	Luxemburg	3
Eire	5	Newfoundland	3
Finland	5	Southern Rho-	3
Netherlands	5	desia	

95

In the extremely unlikely event of all the votes for
Germany, France and the United Kingdom being cast
in a *bloc*, they would amount to less than one-quarter of
the House. On the other hand, the "neutral" powers of
Western Europe (including Eire) would require only
two more votes to give them a majority.

The method of election should, I think, be left to the
States. There are three possibilities:

(1) election by the people;
(2) election by the State legislatures;
(3) appointment by the State Governments.

Of these, I prefer the second. The first tends to give the States' House equal authority with the People's House, which I do not contemplate for reasons explained later. The third would cause many difficulties. There would be a tendency to appoint "superannuated" politicians whose usefulness in federal politics had long since disappeared. State Governments, too, would be apt to appoint members of their own parties instead of providing for proportional representation of all parties. Members of the States' House would tend to regard themselves as representatives of the State Governments, and act accordingly. On the other hand, changes in State Governments would tend to make the position of their nominees very anomalous; and if the nominees resigned when a Government resigned, the representation of some States would be in constant flux. I therefore prefer election by proportional representation by the State legislatures. Such representatives could speak for the different parties in their States, without speaking for the Government; on the other hand, they would not have the same authority as the members of the People's House, who would be direct representatives of the people.

In most respects the States' House would have equal power with the People's House. The result would produce deadlock, in the sense that legislation passed by the lower House might be rejected by the upper House. Readers who have the House of Lords in mind should remember, however, that elected representatives can be thrown out at the next election, whereas hereditary peers go on for ever. If the British members of the States' House obstructed legislation desired by the British members of the People's House, the question would be an issue at the next parliamentary election, and the British Government might be overthrown on this issue. If, however, the smaller States opposed legislation carried in the People's House by the votes of the larger States, this would be the kind of conflict which the States' House was actually set up to create.

The authority of the States' House would not extend, however, to the overthrow of the Federal Government. We must assume Coalition Governments. We must, therefore, assume Governments with not all the strength that British Governments with parliamentary majorities possess. It is most undesirable that they should be further weakened by a dual responsibility to both Houses. We might then reach a position in which no Government could be established, because one Government had no majority in the People's House and its successor had no majority in the States' House. The provision necessary for this purpose is discussed below.

Those familiar with the working of parliamentary government will be aware, however, that responsibility to the People's House alone might not be achieved if the States' House had the power, in the traditional British phrase, to "refuse supplies". Such a refusal of supplies is commonly regarded as the ultimate sanction of responsible government in Great Britain. In any case, financial legislation differs fundamentally from other legislation. If other legislation is not passed, the Government cannot exercise the functions proposed to be con-

ferred by it, and there is the end of the matter. If supplies
are refused, however, there can be no Government at
all. Accordingly, I have provided means in Article VII
of my draft whereby a "money Bill" (which I have
defined along the lines of the Parliament Act, 1911) can
be passed over the heads of the States' House. Realising
the problem created in the British Parliament by the
interpretation of "money Bill" and not being sure that
the People's House will have a Chairman with the same
impartiality as the Speaker, I have given the interpre-
tative function to the Chief Justice of the Federal
Supreme Court.

§ 4. The Federal Government.

Our discussion so far in this chapter leads to the conclusion that we should recommend the establishment of
a "Cabinet" or Council of Ministers responsible to the
People's House. For this purpose it is necessary to have
some comparatively impartial person to set the machinery
in motion, like the sovereign in the constitutional mon-
archies and the presidents of the republics. His essential
function would be to choose a Prime Minister. In the
United Kingdom this function is rarely of importance
because under the two-party system it is clear that the
leader of the parliamentary majority must be Prime
Minister. Where there are several parties, none with a
majority, however, the function is one of some delicacy,
and requires such an appreciation of the political situation that a reasonably stable government can be formed.
Moreover, political leaders who are reluctant to enter a

coalition can often be persuaded if an impartial person of standing appeals to their patriotism and emphasises the principle of the Duke of Wellington's famous phrase: "The King's Government must be carried on."

It is unlikely that the nations would consent to allow any existing head of a State to exercise this function, so we must provide for an elected President. Owing to the tendency of responsible governments to instability, some democratic countries have given their King or their President fairly wide powers, especially in case of emergency. Generally speaking, I do not think that they have been a success, and in some cases—Germany, for instance—they have been catastrophic. In respect of the Federation there are strong reasons for limiting the President's function to a minimum. So long as strong national patriotisms prevail, no nation will have any great confidence in a President who may be drawn from any one of twenty nations. We could not produce a President having in the Federation the reputation of President von Hindenburg—and in any case he set a precedent that nobody wants to follow. Also, no nation will wish to diminish in any way the prestige of the head of their State. British people, for instance, will be anxious not to interfere in any way with the allegiance which they owe to their King.

On the other hand, it is necessary to create a federal patriotism, and for this purpose it is useful to have a figurehead who can become the focus of that patriotism. The President should thus exercise what Walter Bagehot called the "dignified" functions of the Federation. He should be the official head of the Federation, he should theoretically command the armed forces, he should send and receive ambassadors, sign formal documents, and the like, though always on the advice, as we call it —that is, the instructions—of the Council of Ministers. I have provided for him in the draft no independent function except the appointment and (subject to qualification) the dismissal of the Prime Minister, and one power in respect of the dissolution of the Federal Legislature.

The President would thus occupy much the same status as the President of the French Republic. I have therefore suggested (Article V) that he should be elected by the two Houses of the Legislature in joint session. In view of the many nationalities involved and the desirability of his not obtaining a position which infringes the status of the head of a State, I have suggested a three-year term of office only. For the same reason, I have left the State legislature to fix his precedence. I contemplate that in the United Kingdom he would be given a precedence next after the Sovereign.

His primary function (Article VI) would be to appoint a Prime Minister. Other ministers would then be appointed by him at the request of the Prime Minister. We assume a system of responsible government. It is not necessary, I think, that this should formally be embodied in the Constitution. I have, however, provided that the President, acting in his discretion, may dismiss the Prime Minister if a resolution to that effect has been passed by the People's House. This implies also, on the principle known to English law as *inclusio unius exclusio alterius*, that he cannot be dismissed by the President in other cases, though he can of course resign. This in my view is the British rule, though others have sometimes expressed a contrary opinion.

§ 5. The Dissolution of the Legislature.

I have provided for the Legislature (Article VIII) a maximum period of five years, which experience has shown to be reasonable. Most legislatures have three or four years, which is apt to be short in a large unit like the Federation, and I should definitely oppose a period so short as the two-year period of the American House of Representatives. While it is theoretically true that frequent "appeals to the people" cannot be undemocratic, the appeal must be based on work accomplished, and a two-year period, or even a three-year period, means that representatives must spend an unduly long time in nursing their constituencies. Nor must we forget that elections may be expensive for representatives, and that anything that makes membership costly diminishes the range of possible candidates.

Where a right of dissolution is granted, a period of five years becomes, even under the two-party system, a period of four years or even less. Governments do not wait until the period expires by law, lest they be passing at that moment through a temporary unpopularity. They choose a moment before the end of the legal period when they appear to be at the summit of their popularity. In the United Kingdom, for instance, we have had general elections in 1918, 1922, 1923, 1924, 1929, 1931 and 1935. It is of course arguable whether a right of dissolution should be conferred. We have it in the United Kingdom, but most other democratic countries (outside the British Commonwealth) do not permit it. I am strongly of the opinion that it is very desirable. Democratic Governments are apt to be weak, especially where they must inevitably be coalitions. They are at the mercy of chance majorities in the legislature, whose members have little of the sense of responsibility which office confers. A vote is one among many, but if there are enough votes the Government is destroyed without anyone being able to place the responsibility upon the right persons and to sit in judgment upon them. Many French authorities consider that the requirement of Senate consent as a preliminary to dissolution—which means in practice that the legislature is never dissolved—is the fatal weakness of the present French Constitution. The Government, to adapt a phrase of Canning's, should be able to defy a majority and appeal to the people. The policy of the Federation would be the policy of the Government, and it should be possible for the people to express an opinion on that policy, not merely by voting for X or Y at intervals of five years, but by determining, by voting for X or Y, whether the Government should or should not be thrown out. I am perfectly certain that the success of the British system rests in very large measure on the power of the Government to dissolve Parliament if it thinks that public opinion is not properly represented by the House of Commons.

Some would prefer to give the President a complete discretion in the matter. Some have alleged, indeed, that in the United Kingdom the King has power either to compel or to refuse a dissolution. Actually, no Sovereign has compelled a dissolution since the Reform Act of 1832 and, even if he had the power (which I am sure he has not) its exercise would be very dangerous. When this question was discussed in 1913, Liberal leaders pointed out that if the King dissolved Parliament over Home Rule they would fight the election not on Home Rule but on the King's power. In actual fact, the King could not have dissolved Parliament, though he could have dismissed the Liberals and brought in a Unionist Government, which would have advised dissolution. If he had done so he would have been branded throughout the country as a Unionist King, and he had the good sense not to do anything of the kind. An independent power of this character, in other words, would destroy the impartial character of the President's office and would be dangerous to the stability of the Federation.

A power to *refuse* a dissolution is in a different category. It is true that no Sovereign in the United Kingdom has effectively refused a dissolution since 1832 (though it was postponed on the King's insistence in 1910). Nevertheless, it has always been recognised that there is a right to refuse, and such refusals have not been uncommon in the Dominions (the latest was in South Africa in 1939). One can imagine circumstances in which a Government requested dissolution for purely party ends, and when it was perfectly easy to secure a

Government which could control a majority. Suppose, for instance, a Coalition Government supported by the Black, Green and Purple parties, and opposed by the Red and Pink parties. By a majority it agrees upon a policy to which the Purple party is opposed, and that party goes across and joins the Opposition. It may be that the Legislature has been in existence for less than a year. Ought not the President to try to form a Red, Pink and Purple coalition before accepting a dissolution? I think so: and accordingly I have provided (Article VIII, section 2) that the President may grant or refuse a dissolution, but may not dissolve except at the request of the Council of Ministers. It will be noticed that I insist on the advice of the Council of Ministers and not of the Prime Minister. In this country the Prime Minister's power dates from 1918 only, and the recent South African example shows that a Prime Minister who has lost the support of a majority of his own Cabinet ought not to be able to override the Cabinet.

CHAPTER VI

THE FEDERATION AND THE STATES

§ 1. Relations in General.

The Federation is intended to be a union for defined purposes only, which may be brought under the headings of Colonies, Foreign Affairs, Defence and Economic Relations. In other respects, the independence and organisation of the federated States would remain untouched. Nothing would affect the position of the King, for instance, in relation to the United Kingdom, the Dominions, India, or the British Empire. He would still be "of Great Britain, Ireland, and the Dominions beyond the Sea, King, Emperor of India". Similarly, the powers of Parliament would be restricted only so far as the Federal Legislature acquired powers or the Constitution imposed limitations. The relations between the King, the Cabinet, Parliament and the people would remain unaltered. So far as was necessary, I have so provided in my draft (Article XI, section 3), where it is set out that "the powers not exclusively vested in the Federal Legislature nor withdrawn by it from the federated States may continue to be exercised by the federated States". This is what is usually known as the "residue" clause. The residue is intended to remain with the States. Moreover, the residue here is much larger than has been provided in any federal constitution at present in existence.

I have not even contemplated changes in nationality law. In all federations powers relating to nationality and naturalisation are conferred upon the federation. In this case it does not appear to me to be necessary. British subjects would in any case remain subjects of the King, though they would become federal citizens as well. Without losing their national patriotism and their loyalty to the Crown, they would acquire also a federal citizenship. They would remain loyal subjects and yet become good Europeans. It is unlikely that Europeans will reach the position of citizens of the United States and Switzerland, or of British subjects in Canada or Australia, where the federal loyalty is the essential and the State loyalty only incidental. Accordingly, I have in Article IV of my draft left power over nationality and naturalisation to the States. In other words, who are British subjects would be determined by the British Parliament after the British and Dominion Governments had reached agreement. British subjects (except where a Dominion is not a federated State) would be federal citizens because they were British subjects.

I have, however, provided for the transfer to the Federation of the power to issue passports because I contemplate that the Federation would control migration, and the passport system is incidental to such a control. Further, it becomes necessary to provide that a federal citizen in a "foreign" State should have most of the rights of a citizen of that State. This is, of course, the British practice, except where a foreigner is given only conditional entry into the country. It would not be suggested that he could take part in ordinary political activity, nor is it unreasonable to limit the rights of persons who are mere birds of passage. On the other hand, he ought not to be prevented from owning land, carrying on business, or suing in the State Courts. Some countries (usually not democratic countries) have restrictions of this character, but it would be incompatible with the status of a federal citizen and with the Federation's control of migration to impose such restrictions upon him.

A few restrictions of this character, and the transfer of powers to the Federation, necessarily impose some limits on State action. Federation is proposed, indeed, because these limits are considered desirable. We cannot render ourselves secure against German aggression without rendering Germany secure against British aggression, however little we think the need to arise. The Federal Constitution and federal laws would thus override State constitutions and State laws, though only so far as there was repugnancy between them. The Federal Constitution becomes, in the technical phrase, the "supreme law" of the Federation (see Article II of the draft). An Act of Parliament would be invalid if it infringed the Federal Constitution or any provision of a valid federal law.

There is thus a division of powers between the States and the Federation, determined by the Constitution, though most of the powers would in fact be vested in the States. The courts would refuse to apply a federal law if it conflicted with the Constitution, and would refuse to apply a State law if it conflicted with the Constitution or with a valid federal law. In the last resort the question would be determined by the Federal Supreme Court which is recommended in Chapter x.

The result is that necessarily a federation is a "lawyer's paradise". Disputes arise not only under the law but about the law. The first question for a lawyer becomes not "has my client broken the law?" but "is the law which my client is alleged to have broken really a law?" The judges are called upon to undertake very difficult pieces of interpretation. The Constitution necessarily uses very general phrases framed long before anyone could imagine the circumstances to which they could be applied. Provisions drafted in 1787 have had to be applied by the Supreme Court of the United States to the very different conditions of to-day. Even Canada shows the same difficulty, because modern Dominion status was quite inconceivable to those who drafted the British North America Act in 1867. Moreover, the United States Constitution contains some very vague phrases indeed, like "due process of law".

Further, legal proceedings are often not taken until long after a law has been passed. The law is passed by the legislature, and most people then obey it. One person, however, breaks it, and finds legal proceedings taken against him in consequence. His lawyer gets to work, and thinks he can challenge the validity of the law. Accordingly, the legal mills begin their slow grinding and finally, perhaps years later, the law is decided to be invalid. In the meantime, people do not know whether or not to obey the law, because they do not know whether it is a law or not.

In some degree, these are inevitable difficulties of federation, and they must be set off against the advantages to be obtained in other ways. I believe, however, that in some cases they can be overcome. I have suggested in Chapter IV that certain kinds of State legislation for Colonies might be "disallowed" by the Federal Government. This means that within a certain period of the enactment of the legislation—I suggest three months (Article XII)—the Council of Ministers might authorise the President to issue a proclamation which would from that date nullify the legislation. I suggested this procedure in relation to Colonies because it enabled me to propose that Colonies be left with the States subject to restrictions in the interest of the Federation that could be enforced by disallowance. The division of powers which I contemplated was not one which could be interpreted by judges.

Power to nullify State legislation is a very substantial power, and I should not propose its general application. Where it is applied, however, it not only allows the States to exercise powers, subject to disallowance, which might otherwise have to be transferred to the Federation, but also enables the difficulties of judicial review to be overcome. It is possible to provide—and I have so provided in Article II of my draft—that a State law shall not be declared void merely because it conflicts with the Constitution, if the President had a power of disallowance. If the President has disallowed the law, judicial proceedings are unnecessary. If he has not disallowed it, there can be no federal objections to the law even if it does infringe the Constitution. The scope of judicial review is thus narrowed, and the scope of State legislation correspondingly widened

Naturally, the courts might have to determine whether the President had a power to disallow. We could not permit the Federal Government to be the interpreter of its own powers: but in the great majority of cases the power to disallow would be clear and would not be challenged. However, we cannot entirely avoid "judicial review", as it is called. Nor do I suggest that the President should have a general power to disallow legislation which infringed the Constitution, partly because he might then disallow legislation which did not, and partly because we should still have judicial review in connection with his disallowance.

The remedy of disallowance is a remedy to meet special classes of difficulties. The cases are discussed in various passages of this book. There is, however, one special class of case to which reference should be made in this chapter.

§ 2.   The Maintenance of Democracy.

Reasons are given in Chapter II for suggesting that the Federation must be composed of democracies and of democracies alone. What protection have we that all the federated States will remain democratic? At present we have none, though it must be remembered that it would be much more difficult to establish a dictatorial State

within a free federation than it is for a Sovereign State
to pass under the fist of a dictator. It is at once seen that
this problem is a problem of maintaining certain fundamental rights which are essential to a democratic system
—free elections, freedom of speech, freedom of assembly,
freedom of the press, freedom to form political parties,
freedom to establish broadcasting systems or, alternatively, impartial control—and the like.

It is necessary to preserve these within the States
because without them federal elections within a State
would be a farce. "Election by acclamation" as it is
practised in Italy and (presumably) Russia is not election
at all. The right to answer "Yes" or "No", even without
the implied threat of the concentration camp, is not a
right to determine the aims and means of government.
Our federal system implies free democracy within the
States. Some, indeed, would go further. They urge that
it is the business of Western Europe to see that the
decencies of civilisation are maintained, that we should
insist upon trial by jury, habeas corpus, impartial judges,
law-abiding police forces, the suppression of Gestapos
and Ogpus, and the like.

Our approach to this problem must be, I think, from
the federal angle only. The fewer sources of controversy
there are, the more likely are we to achieve federation.
The time and energy devoted to discussing habeas corpus
and trial by jury would be time and energy devoted to
an interesting subject, but would not be devoted to
federation. Moreover, we propose to leave the criminal
law and its enforcement to the States: if at the same time

we impose serious limitations on the States we shall introduce a new element of confusion and further decrease effective State powers.

How, then, are we to prevent such interference with liberty as will hinder the effective operation of federal institutions? The obvious remedy is the insertion of a "Bill of Rights" designed to protect such fundamental liberties. It is the obvious remedy because it has been adopted in the United States. There are, however, serious difficulties. The first is in drafting. The common phrase is that we believe in "liberty but not licence". That means that we believe in liberty subject to restrictions. We believe in liberty of speech, but (in England) subject to the law of libel, slander, blasphemy, sedition, incitement to disaffection, treason, and the like. We believe in freedom of assembly, subject to the law of highways, parks, public order, unlawful assembly, rout, riot, and treason. In a word, we believe that restrictions on liberty should be *reasonable*.

It is not possible to draft a Bill of Rights to give the liberty that is necessary and yet to allow restrictions which are reasonable, unless the terms used are very general. If the terms are general, the interpretation will depend largely on the judges' subjective notions. One man's reason is apt to be another's unreason. Moreover, the idea of reasonableness changes according to conditions. "D.O.R.A." would have been unreasonable in time of peace but was reasonable in time of war. The provisions of the Defence Regulations which the House of Commons regarded as unreasonable a few months ago may be considered to be necessary in a few months' time. In other words, reasonableness is not a test which can easily be applied by judges and, let us say, a Socialist judge might take a different view from a Conservative judge. Judges, however, have no business to be either Socialists or Conservatives. If their functions involve a jurisdiction in which their social or political bias becomes important, the esteem in which they are held will be diminished and the authority of the law depreciated.

Moreover, judicial review in these cases is not always adequate. Let us suppose that X is arrested for a speech in Trafalgar Square, advocating the admission of the Soviet Union to the Federation. He is sent to gaol for six months under an Act of the British Parliament designed to prevent the propagation of communism. He asks for a case to be stated for the opinion of the High Court whether the Act is invalid under the Federal Constitution. If the decision goes against him he may (let us assume) appeal to the Federal Supreme Court. The Court holds the law invalid in so far as it relates to the propagation of communism (or any other "ism") for federal purposes. By this time, twelve months will probably have elapsed, and the man has already served his six months—or, (what is worse) been remanded in custody pending the result of the appeal.

For these reasons, I do not recommend a Bill of Rights in the Constitution. There is, however, a stronger case for the insertion of a Bill of Rights in the preamble. It would then have no legal effect. State legislation contrary to it would not be invalid, but the document would

be quoted in debates in the State and Federal Legislatures, and breaches of it would form the basis of protests
by the Federation to the State. Though this is not in the
British tradition, other nations appreciate the importance
of "unenforceable" rights of this character. Many
written Constitutions include provisions of this kind, and
the famous Declaration of the Rights of Man attached
to the French Constitution of 1791 is really in a similar
position. It was not re-enacted in the constitutional laws
of 1875 which govern the third republic, but it is considered by French lawyers to be implicit in the French
constitutional system.

General statements of this character are not unim-
portant. They provide a standard of reference by which
legislative proposals can be criticised. Especially where
they have become embodied in the national tradition,
as in France, they form a body of doctrine to which
public opinion can rally. If similar statements were
embodied in a federal Constitution, they would form a
basis for representations by the Federation to a State and
a basis for political opposition inside a State. It is, however, doubtful whether this is enough or whether the
advantages would be sufficiently great to overweigh the
difficulties of securing an agreed draft.*

It must be remembered that our scheme contemplates
that all armed forces in the Federation (except possibly
in special cases in colonies) would be vested in the

* There is a further technical difficulty. According to the
law of many States a provision in a preamble is a sub-
stantive enactment.

Federation. In the last resort, the enforcement of laws rests on force. The State would have police forces, but it would have no troops. In the event of serious resistance on the part of a section of its population, it would have to call for the assistance of the Federation. Article III of my draft contains an undertaking by the Federation to assist a State in the maintenance of public order. Now, if the State enacted laws to suppress an opposition or to interfere with free elections, it is certain that the minority would resist, whether by "non-co-operation" or even by rioting (armed resistance would not be practicable), and the laws could not be enforced unless the Federal forces were brought into action. It is arguable that a limitation of the federal guarantee to the effect that federal forces would not be used to enforce laws contrary to a Bill of Rights would be enough. It would then be impossible for a State to proceed to such extreme measures as would in fact interfere with federal elections. However, I feel that this also is not enough. If political opposition in a State were illegal, and were suppressed as far as it could be by ordinary police action, a good deal of it would disappear. Only the more intransigeant elements would continue in operation, and the election of these elements to the People's House would cause riotous scenes in that House that we should do well to avoid. Nor would this method allow a fair representation in the States' House. Further, what is to be feared is not so much a *coup d'état* by which one party seized the government and suppressed its opposition as a gradual encroachment on political liberty which would, over a long period, result in the elimination of opposition political doctrines. Only in the last resort would federal intervention be necessary, and by that time it would be too late.

I consider that the method of disallowance is the key to the solution. If the President has power to disallow laws which might tend to interfere with the holding of free elections, the question of enforcement would not arise. Nor would it be necessary to draft a Bill of Rights. In Article XII, section 2, I have provided a power of disallowance over any law which, in the opinion of the Council of Ministers:

(a) tends to interfere with the freedom of elections to the People's House;
(b) tends to prevent the formation or constitutional operation of political parties having federal objects; or
(c) is likely to require the performance by the Federation of its obligations under Article III.

This provision is strictly relevant to federal purposes. It does not interfere with State legislation more than is necessary. It does not involve judicial interpretation of wide and vague phrases—indeed, it does not require judicial interpretation at all, because the Council of Ministers is the judge. Wider powers could be included if the States would agree, but I doubt if they would accept such further limitations of their sovereignty.

CHAPTER VII

DEFENCE

Of all the objects for which federation is proposed, by far the most important is to render war among the nations of Western Europe absolutely and literally impossible. Complete disarmament is not practicable unless all the nations of the world disarm, and even if that could be achieved war potential would remain. Proportional disarmament, if world-wide, would merely mean that the trained forces and armaments immediately available would be reduced, while leaving war potential unaltered. The one solution is to forbid absolutely the possesssion of armed forces or armaments to Western nations individually, while making them so strong collectively that they would be safe against aggression from outside. The armed forces and armaments required for this purpose would be but a fraction of the forces and armaments maintained in 1938, which were designed primarily to defend the Western nations against each other.

It is a cardinal point of our proposal, therefore, that defence power should be transferred to the Federation. From the constitutional angle, there are no serious difficulties. I suggest no special device. The command of the armed forces of the Federation would be vested in the President, to be exercised, like the rest of the President's powers, by the Council of Ministers responsible to the People's House. The cost would be provided out of federal taxation by legislation, passed annually, presumably, by the Legislature (Article XV). War would be declared by the President, though support by the Legislature would obviously be necessary. Here as in many other matters the system of responsible government operates simply and with adequate checks.

The transitional steps would involve the transfer to the Federation of such State forces as the Federation required. The earliest activities of the Council of Ministers and the Legislature would be concerned with the determination of the nature and size of the forces required. Presumably, the Federation would take over bodily whole divisions of troops, squadrons of air forces, and sections of the fleets. They could no doubt be taken over on an entirely voluntary basis. I do not think that conscription in time of peace would be necessary. The officers and men taken over would not lose their nationality, but would transfer their allegiance for military and naval purposes: that is, they would obey orders given on behalf of the President and would no longer obey orders given on behalf of State Governments. Those who had chosen a military or naval career would find that career open to them in the federal service: those who were fighters temporarily or by compulsion would go back to civil life. Constitutional arrangements for this purpose are not required, since the necessary provisions would be enacted in federal laws.

From the moment when federal forces were ready,

DEFENCE   103

State forces would be disbanded. In Article XV of my draft I have given twelve months for the completion of this transitional stage. Thereafter, no federated State would keep an armed force unless the Federation had authorised a colonial force on the lines discussed in Chapter IV, and set out in Article XVI, section 8, of the draft. It would be necessary for the States to maintain police forces, and recent European experience shows that armed police forces may easily become a danger to neighbouring States. I have, however, met this difficulty by Article XV, section 6, which authorises the President to disallow State legislation which is inconsistent with the Article.

A State which had a trained police force or a large number of pilots trained for civil aviation, or a large mercantile marine, might easily become dangerous if it had reserves of armaments, especially guns, tanks, military aircraft, and warships. My draft includes equipment and other implements of war within "armed forces", so that such of them as were required by the Federation would be transferred, and the rest destroyed. Moreover, the federal forces would be more than a match for untrained forces recruited by a State which had decided to make war on the Federation or on another State. Such a State would no doubt hope to split the federal forces by an appeal to the national patriotism of some of their officers and men. If discipline is maintained among the federal forces, civil war is absolutely impracticable. To meet the remote possibility, however, it is desirable that all equipment and other implements of war should be under federal control. I have therefore provided in Article XV, section 3, that as from the establishment of the Federation no such equipment or implements shall be manufactured in or imported into the Federation except under federal licence. The federal power of disallowance, too, applies generally, so that no State law could authorise fortifications or the establishment of reserves of armaments, or the training of armed forces.

The result would be that within one year the Maginot and Siegfried Lines and all other fortifications within the Federation, including Gibraltar, would be dismantled or taken over. The naval harbours of Great Britain, France, Germany and other powers, including those of Malta, Brest, Heligoland and Cuxhaven, would be taken over. The German and French armies and the British and French navies, among others, would as such completely disappear, though most of the professional soldiers and sailors would find a career open to them in the federal service. The only air force would be the federal force. Though the federal budget would probably be substantial, it would be only a fraction when compared with the combined peace-time budgets of the Western powers. National conscription would disappear overnight, and national energy diverted to peaceful pursuits.

CHAPTER VIII

FOREIGN POLICY

§ 1. External Relations.

Responsibility for defence inevitably carries with it responsibility for foreign affairs. The Federation cannot control the use of armed forces without also controlling the policy which determines when, if ever, those forces are to be used. Accordingly, direct political relations between the federated States and foreign countries must cease, foreign policy will be in the hands of the Council of Ministers, and the President will send and receive ambassadors. Moreover, it is proposed in the next chapter that responsibility for external commerce, migration, air traffic, and navigation and shipping shall be transferred to the Federation, so that commercial treaties as well as political treaties would come within the jurisdiction of the Federal Government.

There are, however, many subjects of international discussion which would be entirely within the jurisdiction of the federated States. They might include, for instance, public health, extradition for the purposes of the criminal law, the mutual enforcement of civil judgments, bankruptcies, patents, trade marks, copyrights, postal and telegraphic services, broadcasting, and the like. In most federations nearly all these subjects come within federal jurisdiction. Since it is not proposed that all of them should be transferred to the Federation, it is reasonable that federated States should have relations with each other and with foreign governments, and relations with which the Federation would not be directly concerned.

In most federations, the federal control over external affairs is complete. But, even where the State powers are narrow, this leads to difficulties. The United States overcomes them because treaties made by the President with the consent of two-thirds of the Senate become part of the law of the United States. Such treaties may deal with matters within the exclusive jurisdiction of the States. This is, however, a severe limitation upon State power of particular importance now that international agreements cover so large a field of ordinary domestic activity, and I doubt whether the States of the European Federation would accept it. On the other hand, if the Federation has the treaty-making power and the States have the legislative power, there is nobody capable of signing an effective agreement. In Canada, for instance, the treaty-making power is in the hands of the Dominion, but the Dominion Parliament has no power (subject to one immaterial qualification) to give effect to such treaties as relate to matters within the jurisdiction of the Provinces.

If the federated States make treaties, however, other difficulties arise. Such treaties, though dealing with matters within the sole jurisdiction of a State, may raise political difficulties of a federal order (for instance, treaties giving aliens of a certain class preference over aliens from another country as to the holding of land, the licensing of businesses, etc.). Further, if a federated State does not carry out its obligations, a foreign State might be induced to take diplomatic action, perhaps leading to war; and such action would inevitably be against the Federation. On the other hand, a federated State could not take diplomatic action against a foreign State except through the Federation.

For these reasons it seems to me that, on the one hand, the States should have a limited treaty-making power and, on the other hand, that the Federation should have control over the exercise of that power. The suggestions in Article XIII are intended to carry out this principle.

(1) A federated State should be able to make agreements with foreign countries on subjects prescribed by the Federal Legislature: and, until that is done, it should be able to make agreements on any subject not within the exclusive jurisdiction of the Federal Legislature.

(2) In order that such treaties shall not raise political issues, either in respect of their contents or because of their subsequent enforcement, they should be signed on behalf of the Federation as well as on behalf of the State. In this way, both State and Federation accept obligations, and the Federation acquires a right to complain if the foreign country does not carry out its bargain. This is taken from the Swiss example.

(3) The Federal Legislature should have power, concurrently with the State, to enact the necessary legislation. Normally, I think it would not do so. It would leave the State legislature to enact the necessary laws because the members of the Federal Legislature (especially of the States' House) would not desire an invasion of the State's field unless it were considered to be really necessary. Nevertheless, if the State did not enact the

laws necessary to carry out its obligations, the Federation could do so, and thus satisfy the complaints of the foreign power.

(4) I suggest that all this should apply to existing treaties. Obligations which related solely to functions transferred to the Federation would become obligations of the Federation. For instance, the obligations of the United Kingdom to defend Portugal, Iraq and Egypt would become federal obligations. Obligations relating to matters within the State jurisdiction, such as those arising under Postal and Telegraphic Conventions, Extradition Treaties, the Drug Traffic, and so on, would remain State obligations, but the Federation would acquire power to enact the necessary legislation.

(5) I include within the last paragraph the moral obligation of the United Kingdom to defend the Dominions, so that the Federation would immediately acquire the duty to defend any Dominion which did not become a federated State. On the other hand, I do not think that the ordinary political arrangements (dealing with such matters as the succession to the Throne, British nationality, appeals to the Privy Council, and so on) between members of the British Commonwealth of Nations, should become of federal concern. Accordingly, I have excluded them in the draft.

§ 2. Relations between Federated States.

Treaties and other arrangements between federated States and dealing with matters coming within federal jurisdiction obviously disappear when the Federation is set up, nor would such treaties or arrangements be made after its establishment. It might be a matter of dispute as to how far the existing treaties remained in force, so in Article XIV, section 3, of the draft I have provided for their continuance until they are abrogated by the parties or declared invalid by the Federal Legislature. I assume that at an early stage of its career the Federal Legislature would have placed before it a Bill containing a schedule of abrogated treaties and parts of treaties.

Treaties between federated States do not give rise to such difficulties as would arise over treaties with foreign powers. There would be no possibility of diplomatic action and no great difficulty of enforcement. My draft (Article XIV, section 1) therefore provides only that such treaties must not be within the exclusive competence of the Federal Legislature. It would be convenient if federal signature were attached, so that the Federal Government could make representations if the treaty were undesirable politically or if it trenched upon federal powers. This is not essential, however, since State legislation under the treaty would be declared invalid by the courts if it went outside the State legislative power.

There is, however, a strong case for giving the Federal Legislature power to legislate with the consent of the parties. It may be noted that any dispute arising out of such a treaty would be within the jurisdiction of the Federal Supreme Court under Article XXII of my draft. There would be additional security if the parties agreed to federal legislation. Moreover, there are many cases where federal legislation would be a much simpler process than concurrent State legislation. International copyright, for instance, requires simultaneous legislation by all the signatories. It would be much more convenient for the terms of an international convention on such a subject to be enacted by the Federation. One would hope that, political differences having been removed, there would be many more such agreements. Indeed, the Federal Government might take the initiative by summoning a Convention for the unification of laws. Once agreement had been reached, federal legislation would save trouble. I have therefore provided the necessary power in Article XIV, section 2, of my draft.

§ 3. International Organisations.

The scheme suggested above, which owes more to the Swiss system than to any other, but is in large part original, requires further consideration of the effect upon present methods of international organisation. There is nothing to prevent the federated States from appointing ambassadors and consuls in foreign countries and in other federated States. The amount of work involved would be small and, except where relations between two States were particularly close, it would generally prove less expensive and more convenient to use the services of the federal diplomatic and consular service. In any case, diplomatic and consular officials sent by federated States should rank lower in precedence than the equivalent federal officials.

International organisations of a purely technical character, dealing only with matters within State jurisdiction (such as Posts and Telegraphs, if not federal) could continue unchanged, though it would be desirable to have a federal representative added. Among these I include the International Labour Office, which deals almost entirely with matters probably of State concern. The League of Nations is in a different category. Its more spectacular functions are essentially federal matters. On the other hand, some of its most effective work has been done in relation to questions of purely State concern. Nothing suggested in this book minimises the importance of the political functions of the League, which would continue to be important outside Western Europe. Nor would the technical functions cease to be important. The recent proposal to separate the two classes would suit admirably the arrangements necessary to meet the consequences of the creation of the Federation. I suggest that only the Federation should be represented on the Council (where it would be, of course, a permanent member and, at present, by far the most important member). There is no reason, however, why the federated States should not be members of the Assembly, it being understood that they would not vote on purely federal matters. The efficacy of the political functions of the League would, of course, depend on its securing the adherence of powers not now members—but that is not a problem of federation.

CHAPTER IX

A EUROPEAN ECONOMY

§ 1. Economic Problems Generally.

A constitutional lawyer must approach economic problems with even more diffidence than he is accustomed to show in relation to ordinary political problems. It is clear on political grounds, however, that economic problems must be faced. However specious be the arguments for *Lebensraum*, it is evident that the nationalist economic control which has developed in Europe, especially since 1931, has been one of the difficulties leading to the present war. The Treaty of Versailles, in its emphasis on self-determination, neglected to provide against the consequent dislocation of economic life. The isolation of Austria, for instance, however explicable on grounds of race or language, could not be justified if, on the one hand, *Anschluss* with Germany was forbidden and, on the other hand, the succession States were enabled to cut off Vienna from the area that it was developed to serve. The solution of the problem of peace necessarily involves a solution of the major economic problems as well.

Moreover, if the Federation is to arouse any enthusiasm it must not be a mere defensive organisation, an instrument designed to meet immediate dangers and likely to collapse if those dangers are removed. It must under-

take positive tasks of reconstruction and social ameliora-
tion. It must not only sweep away the barriers that selfish
nationalism has placed in the path of a general rise in
the standard of living, but also it must assist States and
peoples in the development of a European economy. It
is for this reason that I, personally, would welcome the
delegation to the Federation of very wide economic
powers. Such a process would emphasise the positive
rather than the negative aspect of the Federation. It
would not only establish peace more firmly, but also it
would enable the energy of the peoples of Western
Europe, and particularly the energy which has hitherto
been devoted to competition in armaments, to constructive tasks.

Nevertheless, the immediate question is not what
powers any individual would like to see conferred, but
what powers it is possible to obtain. Here the tentative
character of any proposals which we put forward at
present becomes very clear. The federal solution is unattainable if the nations will not pool their armaments.
If defence powers are transferred to the Federation the
main burden of foreign policy must also be transferred.
I believe that some transfer of economic power follows
inevitably; but I cannot affirm that any particular head
of power must of necessity and inevitably be transferred.
In other words, we are here in a field where negotiation
and compromise are unavoidable, and where one cannot
stand or fall by any particular proposal. Moreover, it is
possible that too ambitious a scheme would do more
harm than good. If it demanded the surrender by States

of too much power it might produce opposition to the
whole idea of federation. For this tactical reason opinion
on this subject has been divided. Some have thought
that the difficulty of securing agreement on economic
matters was so great that it was wise to ask only for the
transfer of defence and foreign policy. Others have
thought that the advantages of freedom of inter-State
trade were so obvious that one might go so far as to
suggest it. A third group of inveterate optimists has
agreed that the advantages of wide federal control are
so great that public opinion could be induced to follow
in large part the examples of the United States, Canada,
Australia and Switzerland.

The answer to this problem depends on the persuasive
skill of economists. It is enough for me to raise the issues
and to provide some kind of draft to form a basis for discussion. The question being so open, I have provided
two drafts. Articles XVIII to XXI confer on the
Federation comparatively narrow economic powers, but
provide also for a reasonable freedom of inter-State
trade. Articles XVIII A and XIX A, on the other hand,
provide for a federal "economic power". It would be
improper for me to express a preference on economic
grounds, though I believe that the weight of expert
opinion falls heavily on the second, or wider power. I
can assert on constitutional grounds, however, that the
second provides many fewer opportunities for political
friction than the first. In other words, constitutional
opinion would agree with economic opinion that
Articles XVIII A and XIX A, though at present even

less mature in form than the rest of the draft, provide a much better solution than Articles XVIII to XXI. If necessary, though I think it undesirable, the powers set out in Articles XVIIIA and XIXA could be cut down, leaving, however, the commerce power which distinguishes this plan from the "Free trade" plan in Articles XVIII to XXI.

§ 2.   Inter-State Free Trade.

No one, I think, has successfully contested the economists' argument that, at least where it is mutual, free trade provides the highest standard of living within the area that enjoys it. It is significant that the first step towards unity taken by any State in the course of its development has been to sweep away *octrois* and other impediments to internal trade. What is good for a unit like France or Germany or Italy is even better for a larger unit like the Federation. It is significant, too, that all existing federations have internal free trade, even where their "protection" against other countries is very considerable. Finally, it is significant that proposals for federation in peaceful conditions have usually begun as proposals for a customs union. Let us not forget, just because we are at war, that Europe has been facing grave economic problems for many years, and that it was universally agreed that a lowering of tariff barriers and the abolition of other restrictions on trade were an essential preliminary. The main difficulty was that each nation wanted the other to begin and, also, wanted an agreement which benefited itself at the expense of its neighbours, just as at the Disarmament Conference every nation wanted to limit armaments of the kind that it did not possess. The universal demand for the lowering of trade barriers had the same effect as the universal demand for restricting armaments, namely, that it increased them. This is the inevitable result of negotiations by independent States, because each is concerned to get ninepence for fourpence. Federation provides an opportunity to solve this problem over a wide area by conferring the necessary authority on the Federation or by restricting the powers of the States. It is, in fact, easier to obtain specific ends as part of a general settlement than to attain them separately. The question to be answered in this preliminary stage is how far public opinion is ready to go.

One preliminary point may be dealt with shortly because it does not raise the general issue. It is clear that each federated State must treat other federated States not less favourably than it treats States outside the Federation. This would apply even to British relations with Dominions outside the Federation. Further, no federated State could be permitted to discriminate among other federated States. It would not be suggested that Belgium should at once extend its customs union with Luxemburg so as to include all other federated States: but other differences of treatment would be regarded as discriminatory, and they would include the "imperial preference" which members of the British Commonwealth of Nations offer to each other. For a different reason, no State would be entitled to discriminate in its colonies and dependencies in favour of itself. Unless the principle of equality of opportunity is applied, there is no case for allowing a State to continue to keep its colonies or, alternatively, there is a strong case for restoring the German colonies.

All this means in practice the generalisation of the "most-favoured nation" clause which is common in commercial treaties, along the lines of Article XVII of the draft. Great Britain commonly includes such a clause in its commercial treaties, so that the provision would affect us primarily by an extension to the federated States of "imperial preference". I do not regard this as serious: trade negotiations like those at Ottawa have tended towards the disruption of the British Commonwealth more than towards its strengthening. Unity depends on sentiment and not on commercial advantages.

This is, however, but a step in the transition from cut-throat economics to collaboration. The essential question is whether to proceed to federal economic unity by way of restriction or by way of the exercise of federal powers. In examining the problem it will be convenient to discuss free trade by restriction first, because probably the process of negotiation and persuasion would be easier.

Free trade within the Federation can be attained by so providing. It could probably not be attained immediately. The free trade argument, as I understand it, concludes that free trade is for the benefit of the population generally. It does not, I think, assert that a particular trade or industry—employees as well as employers—may not benefit from a tariff wall. It is, indeed, part of the case that industries must necessarily benefit unequally, and that political "log-rolling" and "lobbying" of the kind familiar in the United States and familiar to us also since 1932 (though in a more restrained manner) is an inevitable part of a tariff system. There are at present in all States of Western Europe vested interests enjoying advantages at the expense of the generality of people behind tariff walls. Possibly there were good arguments in each case— perhaps of a defence order, and perhaps because other nations imposed duties on exports from the State concerned; I am not prepared to discuss the issues because it is admitted that they are no longer relevant if we strive to make Western Europe into a single economic unit. The only point relevant to us is that a sudden tariff reduction in such cases would create unemployment in that industry in that particular country. It would, of course, create more employment in that industry in other countries, but language and other difficulties would prevent a voluntary migration of labour. It would, also, create more employment in other industries through the increase in the standard of living caused by more economic production. Further, there would be a certain, though small, loss of capital through the wastage of existing plants. Capital, on the other hand, can be transferred much more easily than labour.

The consequences can easily be exaggerated; and in

particular it appears that they would be much less serious if there were a general and contemporaneous abolition of tariffs all along the line and in every country in Western Europe. In other words, general abolition as part of a general settlement is much easier to obtain than reduction or abolition in specific cases. Nor must it be forgotten that the formation of the Federation would coincide with the demobilisation of military forces and the conversion of war industries to production for peace. There is some case for saying that complete free trade immediately on the formation of the Federation would cause less dislocation than a gradual reduction over a transitional period.

However, it is probable that the natural timidity of statesmen, especially in the presence of economic forces which they barely understand, would cause them to adopt what might well be the worse alternative. I have accordingly assumed in my draft (Article XVIII, section 1 ; Article XIX, section 1 ; Article XXI, section 1) a transitional period of 10 years. I cannot justify that figure. I doubt if any figure could be justified. Theoretically, it should accord with the turn-over of labour and capital. My slight acquaintance with these subjects induces me to suggest that it would be different for different industries, different for capital and labour in the same industry, and different for different kinds of labour and for different kinds of capital in the same industry. This, incidentally, is one of the many reasons for advocating the conferment of the necessary powers on the Federation; but we have for the present assumed that a federal "commerce power" might be unattainable. Our present argument assumes the establishment of free trade, after a transitional period, simply by constitutional restriction on the States. In the United States and Canada no period of transition was provided. In Australia the period was two years, except in respect of Western Australia, where it was five years. The tariff weapon is now more potent than it was in 1787, or 1867, or 1900, and I have inserted the figure ten, not because I can defend it, but because it is a good round figure and a figure is better than a blank.

It is not easy, however, to define for legal purposes exactly what one means by "free trade". In its narrowest sense it means the absence of restriction on the import and export of goods. Even here, however, there must be restrictions. In the exercise of what in the United States is called the "police power"—which includes power to regulate the health, morals, safety, and general welfare of the citizens of the State—limitations on commerce may be necessary. If the States retain the power to regulate or control agriculture, for instance, they must have power to prevent the spread of foot-and-mouth disease and other diseases in animals and plants. If the State retains its responsibility for the health of its citizens it must have port sanitary regulations and regulations relating to the passage of diseased persons across the frontier. If the State retains power over the criminal law, it must be able to forbid the entry of noxious drugs, dangerous articles (including explosives), obscene and blasphemous literature, and the like. Nor is it necessarily a question of imports only. Florida, for instance, forbids the export of citrus fruits which are immature or unfit for human consumption, and this has been upheld by the Supreme Court of the United States because it promotes the general reputation and prosperity of Florida. In respect of other powers, too, difficulties may arise. For instance, if a State retains the power of taxing motor vehicles, may it forbid the entry of untaxed vehicles?

This argument implies some qualification on the free trade clause. The difficulty is, however, that the more qualifications of this character that one includes the more nearly the Federation would approach to the "lawyer's paradise". Commerce does not fit nicely into legal categories, and long, costly and troublesome litigation would be necessary, as it often is in the United States. Moreover, it is extremely difficult to determine whether restrictions imposed, as it is alleged, for purposes of public health or for the purpose of preventing free trade are in fact proposed for those reasons. It is at least arguable that the Californian prohibition on the importation of fruit and vegetables is designed to protect Californian agriculturists' profits rather than to keep out disease. This is obviously a case in which disallowance is a better remedy than legal proceedings. A still better method would be to give the Federal Legislature a concurrent power on these matters, federal legislation overriding State legislation; but this would be to approach the commerce clause by means of a list of powers rather than by general definition.

It may be that even a power of disallowance is too wide. In that case, we must fall back on judicial review. At the same time, it is most undesirable that people should be left in a state of doubt whether a law was valid or not. The ordinary judicial procedure takes too long and may operate only after the law has been in force for years. In Article XVIII, section 4, I have therefore given a power of disallowance, but allowed the State to bring the question before the Federal Supreme Court. The law would then not be in operation unless and until the Supreme Court declared that it was validly enacted. I do not like this provision, and I would prefer to leave the power of disallowance without qualification. Nevertheless, it may appear to be a reasonable compromise to those who fear the collection of too great powers in the hands of the Federal Government.

This is by no means the only difficulty attendant upon free trade. We have so far tended to assume that trade, commerce and industry imply free competition. In fact, however, all the States of Western Europe have gone far in the direction of economic control, and it is probable that some of them would come under the control of socialist parties and go very much further in that direction than they have done hitherto. The constitutional scheme in this book is not suggested as a means for protecting capitalism or hindering socialism. Nor, on the other hand, is it suggested as a means for attaining socialism. These are questions that the peoples of the Federation and of the several States may be asked to answer by political parties. What I am concerned with is a Constitution which will allow the peoples to make a choice by electing representatives of the appropriate brand to the appropriate legislatures. If the federal Constitution in effect prohibited socialism, it would collapse if and when a socialist majority was obtained. If, on the other hand, it compelled socialism, it would collapse if and when an anti-socialist majority was obtained. What is wanted is flexibility to meet changing opinions.

Nor does this question arise only when a socialist Government is in control of a State. So-called "capitalist" Governments have established marketing schemes and controlled production and have established Government monopolies. Some States, for instance, have tobacco and liquor monopolies. The problem with a socialist Government is the same, except that it would establish State monopolies for a wider range of commodities. If we think of it in terms of a single monopoly we shall necessarily think of it in terms of a wide range of monopolies.

There is no reason why the State monopoly of tobacco in France, for instance, should not continue. We could not suggest that tobacco grown in Rhodesia, or cigarettes manufactured in England, should then be imported into France free of duty. We should expect Rhodesian tobacco to be treated at least as fairly as Virginian or Turkish tobacco. We should, too, expect that English manufacturers should be on exactly the same basis as French manufacturers. It is not easy to put this into legal form, but I have suggested a form of words in paragraph (e) of section 3 of Article XVIII, to the effect that the State may enact laws

> to enable the federated State to control the production, distribution or supply of any commodity within the State: provided that such a law shall not exclude or substantially interfere with commerce with any other federated State.

Even more clearly than in respect of other limitations on free trade, this is a limitation which should be checked by disallowance rather than by judicial review. We must recognise, however, that it might easily lead to acrimonious disputes between a "capitalist" Federal Government and a socialist State Government. Perhaps, therefore, we should include the safety-valve of judicial review in this case as in other limitations. Accordingly, I have brought this also within the provisions of Article XVIII, section 4, quoted above.

§ 3. Federal Powers and Free Trade.

If inter-State free trade is to be effective, however, more is required than a mere prevention of State tariffs. Tariffs are one only of the many methods now adopted to achieve exclusionist policies. Exchange control, restrictions on the movement of capital, control of investments and banking, quotas of imports and production, subsidies for exports, marketing monopolies, discriminatory transport facilities, and many more weapons are in the armoury of "autarky". Moreover, free trade implies free movement of labour—though language difficulties will always keep this down to a minimum.

I am unable to suggest provisions which, inserted as

limitations on State activity, would satisfactorily prevent "concealed protection" from being as effective as open protection by tariffs. Indeed, I have already admitted, in paragraph (e) of Article XVIII, section 3, an exception to the free trade clause which even permits tariffs to be used as ancillary to these methods. I am therefore compelled to suggest additional federal powers in economic matters.

Moreover, it is, I think, clear that the Federation must control trade outside the Federation. Trade questions are intimately bound up with questions of foreign policy. Also, free trade within the Federation implies federal control of trade outside the Federation. One could not have, say, a 25 per cent tariff on motor cars in Great Britain and a 50 per cent tariff on such motor cars in France but no tariff between Britain and France, because the result would be that all American motor cars would be imported into Great Britain even when they were intended for France. Great Britain would collect all the revenue and France would collect none. Obviously, if there is to be an external tariff, it must be uniform—which means in practice that it must be federal.

The control of trade and commerce outside the Federation implies, too, control of the instruments of that trade. If Belgium, for instance, had lower standards of safety for its ships than Holland, there would be discrimination against Dutch ships. Moreover, the Federal Government might even in time of peace desire to have some regulation of imports and exports, and in time of war the requisitioning and control of shipping and aircraft is an essential defence power. If federal control over foreign trade is to be effective, the Federation must possess all the powers which a State now possesses, because we do not know the methods which the Federation might wish to use. In the case of aircraft there is the further argument that civil aircraft can be converted into bombers in a few hours, and it is essential to our scheme that no State should have control of anything that might be an instrument of aggression.

Nor is internal free trade adequate if the instruments of trade can be used to establish concealed protection. For instance, Great Britain might insist that all goods be imported from the Continent in British ships and aircraft. It might also impose very high transport rates for imported goods and low rates for exports. Thus, in order to prevent cauliflowers from France competing in the London market with cauliflowers from Cornwall it might impose prohibitive railway rates on the carriage of French cauliflowers. That would be just as effective "protection" as a tariff. No doubt some will say that such a scheme would be a very good idea. But if other nations used the same methods for British industrial products Great Britain would send no exports to the Federation. If we assume, as we have done, that free trade is much preferable to this inner-State economic war, we must prevent concealed restrictions as well as obvious ones. Accordingly, I have provided in Article XIX for the exclusive control by the Federation, after the transitional period, of trade and commerce outside the Federation, of navigation and shipping, and of traffic by air.

Most of these arguments apply equally to traffic by rail and road, though they are less obvious to us than they would be, for instance, to a Swiss. Free trade is nullified if, say, the industrial products of the Rhineland are unable to compete in France with the industrial products of the North of France because it costs five times more to send them by rail or road in France. Difficulties have arisen in Australia because the federal control over railways is not ample enough; and the United States and Canada have much wider power over traffic by rail and road. I have not inserted a provision to meet this problem because if a power of this character is added to the others we shall almost have reached a federal commerce power. I draw attention to the very real difficulty, however, and it is one of the reasons for suggesting that a federal commerce power should be conferred.

Much the same line of argument applies to concealed restriction by control of currency and capital movements. Inter-State trade becomes impossible if the means for payment cannot be obtained. If, for instance, I order books from France I am prevented from getting them just as effectively if I cannot get francs to pay for them as I should be if they were stopped at a British port. Even if drastic action of this character were not taken, the use of the State power of control and even the existence of fluctuating currencies might seriously inter-fere with the advantages to be obtained from inter-

State trade. Such restrictions and fluctuations are particularly likely to arise in time of economic distress, which is just the time when the problems should be looked at from a very wide angle.

Accordingly, it seems desirable to confer upon the Federation the powers necessary to control currency and inter-State payments and the transfer of securities. These powers would not be effective without control over banking, or at least over that part of banking which is concerned with inter-State and foreign trade. These are wide powers. They need not go so far as to provide for a single currency. Nor do they necessarily imply that the whole of banking law should be enacted by the Federal Legislature. I have, accordingly, not provided (Article XX) for their exercise by the Federal Legislature exclusively. In so far as there was federal legislation, only State legislation inconsistent with it would be invalid. I have, however, suggested that, if the Federal Legislature so provided, any such power might become exclusively federal. For instance, the first stage might be to provide for the stabilisation of exchange rates through a Federal Bank; the second might be to provide a federal currency in addition to the State currency. Later, it might be considered desirable to abolish the separate State currencies.

I have also included with these powers a power over weights and measures. These are already common over most of the Federation, and the separate Anglo-Saxon system is a nuisance which benefits nobody, though it would also be a nuisance for a short time to change it.

I see no reason why British people should not allow the Federation to establish the metric system; though no one would be particularly unhappy if the British people insisted upon retaining rods, poles and perches as a *sine qua non* of their entry into the Federation.

Finally, I suggest in Article XVIII, section 5, that the Federation should obtain exclusive control over migration to and from the federal territory into Europe. Freedom of movement seems to me to be one of the essential characteristics of a federation. Every existing federation has a common nationality which involves the suppression in fact if not always in form of the individual State nationalities. Our strong national patriotism makes any such measure impossible in Europe, and I have already explained that under Article IV of my draft all State citizens would retain their separate State nationalities, and the States would retain their powers over nationality and naturalization. Nevertheless, I should not feel myself to be truly a federal citizen unless I could travel as freely to France or Germany as I can travel to Scotland. The Federation cannot be based merely on mutual suspicion. The nations must learn to feel their common interests exceed their differences. Leaving control of nationality is already a considerable concession to national particularism, and language provides a bar more effective than any. It seems evident that for psychological reasons alone movement should be free—or at least under federal control.

Economic considerations lead to the same conclusion. Free trade requires free migration because it assumes

JF   5 some mobility of labour. The language bar is sufficiently strong to prevent any large-scale flooding of a country by cheap labour. There is proportionately much more migration from Ireland to England than there would be, for instance, into France from Germany. Any fears that trade unionists may have on this ground should be removed by the greater ease of securing an extension of trade unionism in a federation where example would be contagious. Indeed, it is more than likely that middle-class migration would be more noticeable than working-class migration. The technician and the professional man find less difficulty in living away from their own people. Often, too, they speak at least one language beside their own, so that the period of cultural acclimatisation is less.

Again, we are not in a realm where I am prepared to be dogmatic, but I think that the Federation should have exclusive control of migration in Europe. The difficulty of applying this principle outside Europe is substantial. I do not think that the Dominions would give up their control over immigration. Nor do I think that colonial powers would allow free immigration from Europe into their colonies. These difficulties have already been discussed in Chapter IV. In Article XVIII, section 5, I provide for the transfer to the Federation of powers over migration only so far as Europe is concerned. The Dominions would thus retain their power over immigration. European powers with colonies would also retain control over immigration into their colonies, but here I have inserted qualifications:

(1) Such laws might be disallowed on the advice of the Colonial Commission, and laws already in force might be repealed by the Federal Legislature.

(2) Such laws should not discriminate between federal citizens from different federated States in Europe.

The second of these qualifications seems to me to remove any just complaint founded on the need for *Lebensraum*.

§ 4. A Federal Commerce Power.

I do not pretend that the scheme outlined above is very satisfactory. It would be, I think, much better than the present system of economic anarchy. It would, nevertheless, create many difficulties. There are infinite possibilities of squabbling between the Federation and the States and among the States themselves. It is, too, essentially restrictive and negative in its operation. It would seek to prevent States from taking action rather than to encourage the peoples to meet their economic needs in common. It would tend towards the establishment of economic unity, but only because nobody could effectively stop such a tendency and not because there would be much conscious effort directed to that end. In actual operation it would be much like the earlier American system, because the federal commerce power in the United States was not much used during the first hundred years. This is another case where the historical argument, however, is fallacious. Industrial organisation in Europe has long passed the stage where strict *laissez faire* is practicable, and there is no moving "frontier" allowing for constant expansion, as there was in the United States.

In particular, the scheme does not allow for economic "planning", whether on socialist or on capitalist lines. It is not my purpose to discuss whether either is desirable. What I must be concerned with is that the people of the Federation, and even more likely the people of a State, may elect a socialist majority or some other kind of majority pledged to a planned economy. A constitution which does not enable the people to try experiments which it wants to try is a faulty instrument—just as faulty as a constitution which compelled the Federation to "plan" when the people favoured rugged individualism. A good constitution should enable the people to accept either, or any compromise between them.

The scheme above does not permit either the Federation or a State to carry out a planned economy. The Federation could not do it because it would not have a general commerce power. A State could not do it because in spite of the qualification which I have deliberately inserted in Article XVIII, section 3 (e), the Federation could always insist on free trade. For those who believe that planned economy is necessary to raise the standard of living, to reduce unemployment, or to provide a fair distribution of wealth, the alternatives are to give the States greater freedom or to give the Federation greater power. The former method would not avoid inter-State economic "war", it would detract substantially from the psychological unity of the Federation and would therefore cause friction in the working of the machine, and it would not be entirely successful, especially in a State like Great Britain, the Netherlands, or a Scandinavian country which relies very largely on export trade.

The impression which I have derived from the arguments of economists of various schools is that most of those who favour "planning" start with the assumption that their aims would be better achieved if the economic powers of the Federation were reduced to a minimum, and then after thought and argument they conclude that after all a federal commerce power is desirable. Economists of other schools start with the assumption that a federal power is desirable because it enables purely nationalistic restrictions on free competition to be swept away over a very wide and economically important area. The result is the most astonishing phenomenon of the federal movement, an almost complete agreement among economists, or at least among those who think that federation is in any case necessary in order to prevent war.

On purely constitutional grounds I agree with them. A comparison between Articles XVIII to XXI of the draft, on the one hand, and the Supplementary Articles XVIII A and XIX A, on the other hand, shows how much simpler are the latter—though in fact they contain more than the necessary minimum. It is a useful general proposition, commonly valid, that the simpler the drafting the more easily the Constitution will work. Given a modicum of good will, there is much less cause for friction under the more extensive power than under the more restricted power because the main issues would be fought out in the Federal Legislature, and not in quasi-diplomatic negotiations between Federation and State or between State and State.

I am therefore entirely in favour of some scheme like Articles XVIIIA and XIXA. They involve, however, a substantial surrender of power by the States, and I could understand reluctance to take what appears to be such a long step into the unknown. Actually, it is not such a long step as is implied in Articles XVIII to XXI. It will be noted that only the powers in Article XIXA would be exclusive to the Federation, and these powers are also provided in fact by Articles XVIII and XIX. The powers proposed in Article XVIIIA are concurrent. The Federal Legislature would not exercise them unless there was a majority for that purpose in both Houses. In other words, a majority of the representatives of the people and of the representatives of the States would have to agree before any power under Article XVIIIA was exercised at all. I do not think that such agreement could be obtained quickly or easily. In the meantime the *status quo* would continue, whereas Article XVIII provides for a definite and substantial restriction on State power after ten years. What this really means is that the plan described in the previous section of this chapter would compel people to take a long stride into the unknown, whereas the plan proposed in the present section enables them to feel their way as the idea of federal unity grew, and not to take the step at all if that idea did not grow. As often happens, what appears to be the more radical proposal is in fact the more conservative, especially when it is remembered that both the People's House and the States' House must agree.

The most important power in Article XVIII A is the power—not, it must be repeated, the exclusive power—to make laws relating to trade and commerce between the States and between the Federation and foreign countries. This is taken from the Constitution of the United States, where the Congress has power "to regulate commerce with foreign nations and among the several States". In Australia the Commonwealth Parliament similarly has power to make laws with respect to "trade and commerce with other countries, and among the States". The Canadian Constitution provides simply that the Dominion Parliament may legislate for "the regulation of trade and commerce".

The American and Australian powers have been very widely construed by the courts. To quote in a slightly shortened form from a recent decision of the Supreme Court of the United States, the commerce power is a power to enact all appropriate legislation for the protection and advancement of inter-State commerce, to adopt measures to promote its growth and insure its safety, and to foster, protect, control and restrain. Or, as an Australian judge has put it, it is not limited to the act of transportation across the boundaries of a State, but extends to all the accessory methods in fact adopted by Australians to initiate, continue and effectuate the movement of persons and things from State to State. In

the United States, if not in Australia, the federal legislature may control everything which tends to restrict
the flow of what is called "the stream of commerce"
from State to State, so much so that even the regulations
between employers and employees in an industry producing for inter-State commerce are within the ambit of
the power.

I see nothing objectionable in this, except that the
distinction between inter-State and intra-State commerce
then becomes highly artificial. The fact is that free trade
in the narrowest sense has made the United States an
economic unit in the widest sense, so that all trade and
industry is or is capable of being inter-State. The Pitts-
burgh manufacturer naturally assumes that he will sell
in New York and Illinois, and even in Texas and California, if he can. He does not think of himself as a
Pennsylvania manufacturer any more than the Holly-
wood film producer considers that he is engaged in the
export trade if his films are shown outside California.
The "home market" is anywhere in the United States.

This attitude is the result of a long evolution. The
commerce power in the United States was of very little
importance for a hundred years, except that its existence
prevented the States from interfering, by tariffs or otherwise, with the flow of commerce. Consequently, trade
developed on a continental basis and not within the
narrow bounds of State frontiers and, when the need for
federal control became apparent, the commerce clause
was found to give the necessary power. Western Europe
has already achieved—and in some countries achieved

earlier—the high industrial organisation of the United States, but the "continental" habit of thought has not developed. Free trade alone is not enough, because most Western European States have factory laws, workmen's compensation laws, marketing laws, sickness and un-employment insurance, and other forms of State in-surance and control. In most respects, indeed, industrial legislation in these countries is in advance of thåt of the United States. This is due partly, it must be confessed, to the division of powers betwen the United States and the States. There is a substantial body of opinion which believes that economic unity has now gone so far that State powers ought to be even more rigidly limited.

It should be noted that the phrase "commerce... among the several States" is extremely vague. It has received its wide connotation by progressive judicial interpretation. The Canadian power, "the regulation of trade and commerce", is on its face even wider, because it is not even limited to inter-State trade but would appear to cover intra-State trade as well. In fact, how-ever, it covers almost nothing, because the Provinces were given specific power over "property and civil rights", and the Judicial Committee of the Privy Council has given a wide meaning to "property and civil rights" and a narrow meaning to "trade and commerce". In large part this result was due to a historical accident. "Property and civil rights" was inserted to protect the civil law of Quebec against Anglo-Saxon interference. The first legislation of a commercial character which came before the Privy Council was a Dominion Act which provided for the insertion of clauses in insurance contracts. Any lawyer would say that this was a matter rather of "civil rights" than of "trade and commerce", though in fact it is both. But, having established the precedent, the Privy Council gradually expanded the notion of "property and civil rights" and correspondingly limited the notion of "trade and commerce". The result is, I think, disliked by most Canadians.

I have mentioned this rather technical point because the contrast between the United States and Canada is instructive. It shows that a vague phrase may depend for its meaning on accidental considerations and on the proclivities of judges. Obviously, we ought to give the judges a much better explanation of what we mean by "trade and commerce between the States". Precisely what we do mean depends on the extent to which we are prepared to confer powers on the Federation. Let us remember that we are not proposing that the power shall be exclusive. No power could be exercised unless a majority in the People's House and the States' House agreed. Until that was attained, the States would go on as before. This being so, I should be prepared to confer a very wide power; but I am an enthusiastic federalist, and the actual negotiation will be in the hands not of enthusiasts but of timid statesmen and cynical civil servants. Let us, therefore, try to list the subjects which might possibly be brought within "commerce".

1. Imports and exports—in other words, tariffs, quotas of import and export, and other restrictions actually at the frontier.

2. Transport across frontiers by railway and road (shipping and aircraft are covered by Article XIX A, which in this respect merely repeats Article XIX). If this were not covered, the State could in fact interfere with federal power over imports and exports by means of discriminatory rates and other forms of restriction (such as forbidding through passage of railway cars and motor vehicles).

3. Inter-State banking, inter-State payments and the transfer of securities. In a previous section of this chapter it was explained how a State could, by restrictions on financial transfers, interfere with free trade or—as we now put it—with federal trade policy. We might bring currency control within this head also.

4. Negotiable instruments. This is ancillary to the previous head. Negotiable securities are the normal means of inter-State payments. Possibly they might be regarded as within the previous head, partly for that reason, and partly because they are normally discounted by banks. Nevertheless, it is wise to consider whether a uniform law relating to bills of exchange, cheques and other negotiable instruments might not be very useful to the business community.

5. Company law. Most commerce is carried out through incorporated companies. If a State insisted that only companies with, say, 90 per cent of shareholders of the State's nationality should operate in or trade with the State, inter-State trade would be very substantially interfered with. Nor would it be enough for a federal law under the commerce power to provide for the mutual recognition of State companies. A State could then follow the example of Delaware in making its company law so favourable to companies and so unfavourable to shareholders that companies tended to gravitate towards that State. The Federation might require to

do some "trust-busting", and so it might be wise to confer a specific power over companies.

6. Patents, trade marks and trade designs. Obviously, there should be general regulation of these. The question is whether it is enough to leave it to inter-State agreement, as in the present practice, and to hope that no State will be contumacious, or whether regulation is desirable.

7. Copyrights. The same argument applies here, though we are getting away from "commerce".

8. Communications. The practice here is much the same as for trade marks, patents and copyright. On the whole (except as to broadcasting) the present arrangement works well. But would it not be a considerable advantage commercially, and also assist substantially in the formation of a federal spirit, if the Federation as well as the States had powers?

9. Planning. While the above would be enough for ordinary capitalist and competitive inter-State trade, it would not permit planning, whether by means of socialised industry and commerce, or by planned rationalisation, marketing schemes, and so on. For this purpose, the production and distribution of commodities would need to be under federal control.

10. Conditions of labour. This, too, may perhaps be said to be involved in planning. In any event, there is a case for the conferment of this power where free competition exists. The argument for State tariffs rests, to a substantial degree, on the theory that a State with wide social services, stringent safety requirements and a high wage standard, is at a disadvantage compared with a State which permits "sweated labour". I am not concerned to argue this proposition; but as a majority may well agree with it, it may be desirable to enable the Federation to secure uniform standards, especially because migration is assumed to be under

federal control and sweated "foreign" labour might, theoretically at least, be used for under-cutting wage rates and, perhaps, strike-breaking.

Exactly how many of these powers would be accepted I do not know. I have drafted Article XVIII A so as to include them all except the last, because that seems likely to receive the most criticism and it is simpler to draft an exception with a view to its deletion if thought fit.

The powers proposed in Article XVIII A are concurrent powers. That means that State legislation would be valid so long as it was not "repugnant" or contradictory to federal legislation. It is this fact, as I have explained, which would permit of a gradual assumption of federal power as federal economic unity developed. The Article would be, so to speak, a reserve of power to be drawn on gradually as occasion arose. The interpretation of the Article would rest with the judges, who would also determine whether State legislation was repugnant to federal legislation. There is the further question, however, whether State legislation which was contrary to federal policy ought not to be prevented even if the federal legislature had not covered the field with its own legislation. For instance, it ought to be considered whether the Federation should not have power to prevent a State tariff even where there was no federal tariff. The Federal Legislature could, of course, pass the necessary legislation; but this might take months, during which inter-State trade might be seriously interfered with. I have inserted a provision permitting disallowance, though I recognise the serious interference with State autonomy that it allows.

§ 5. Taxation.

The attentive reader will have noticed that I have said nothing about taxation (except by tariffs) and that the draft Constitution contains no taxation clause. The omission is deliberate. The division of powers of taxation is undesirable, as the experience of Canada and (in a sense) of the United States shows. Taxing legislation is unlike ordinary legislation in that concurrent powers rarely conflict. In some Canadian Provinces the individual pays income tax three times—to the Dominion, the Province and the City—though he should be happy in the reflection that the three taken together form but a fraction of what he would pay to the Commissioners of Inland Revenue if he were in England. Multiplicity of taxes is one of the unavoidable difficulties of federation. It prevents any scientific adjustment of taxation to ability to pay; but as no State in fact has any such scientific adjustment this is theoretical rather than practical. Also, collaboration is often desirable. For instance, there ought not to be two methods of computing "profits" involving a duplication of accounts. These are, however, matters to be considered by the Legislatures, not matters requiring constitutional provisions. The taxing power is to be found in Article XI, section 1, of my draft, where the Federal Legislature has powers "to make such laws as may be necessary and proper for carrying into execution the powers of the

Federation or of the Federal Legislature or other Federal institutions". There is, too, an express reference to taxation in Article VII, section 3, which removes any doubt as to the interpretation. The way in which taxing powers should be exercised ought to be examined, but it is not a problem for the constitutional lawyer.

Nor have I suggested the making of grants to compensate States for their loss of tariff revenue. Such proposals would depend upon the circumstances of different States and the extent to which the removal of the burden of armaments compensates for the loss of revenue. They involve argument which, if the experience of Canada and Australia is any guide, would go on for ever. If grants prove essential, they can be effected by federal legislation, because I have followed the example of the United States Constitution in Article XI, section 2, where I have given the Federation power to spend money for the "general welfare". I hope, however, that this power would be used for specific purposes such as assistance to federal health control, the provision of waterways, and possibly assistance to things like unemployment insurance and education, and would not be used for the making of unconditional grants-in-aid to States.

CHAPTER X

JUDICIAL SETTLEMENT OF DISPUTES

§ 1. The Judicial Power.

The frequent references in this book to "judicial review", to a "lawyer's paradise", and to the choice between judicial invalidation and disallowance, will have already emphasised the importance of the judicial power in a federation. A federal Constitution implies a division of powers between States and Federation according to law; and he who decides the law inevitably decides also the precise division of authority. This result is in large degree unavoidable; government according to law implies in large measure government by judges.

So far as disputes between States are concerned, this result is indeed one of the major purposes of any proposal for federation. Though we have achieved government by law internally, this present war is being waged because government by law has never been established internationally on the same kind of foundation. We are fighting, as statesmen of all parties have said, in order to re-establish the rule of law in Europe. Rule or government by law cannot be placed on a firm foundation unless all disputes are determined by judicial decisions.

For this purpose, the judicial power is not ancillary to the division of powers, a means to achieve other ends; it is an end in itself. One of the first tasks of federation must therefore be the establishment of a Federal Supreme Court charged with the function of deciding all disputes between federated States. The rules to be applied, in so far as they are not included in the Constitution or in federal legislation enacted under powers conferred by the Constitution, would be the rules of international law. For the first time in Europe there would be a tribunal applying to all disputes between federated States the rules which international lawyers have optimistically expressed for centuries. Law, not force, would regulate controversies within the Federation.

The Federation would itself be a new State, and disputes between the Federation and a federated State would similarly fall within the jurisdiction of the Federal Supreme Court. Disputes between the Federation or a federated State, on the one hand, and a non-federated State, on the other hand, would be determined by the existing means—by the League of Nations, the Permanent Court of International Justice, by arbitration, by diplomatic discussion, or, if need be, by war on behalf of the Federation.

These give us two of the items of federal jurisdiction set out in Article XXII, section 1, of the draft Constitution. If the Federation were at war, it would need to have questions of prize determined. Accordingly, this is a third head of federal jurisdiction. Piracy on the high seas similarly seems to be a subject of international character which could be dealt with more effectively by the Federal Supreme Court than by the State tribunals. Finally, the Federal Legislature, in the exercise of any of the powers referred to in preceding chapters of this book, might decide that the Federal Supreme Court was the appropriate body for dealing with disputes.

Questions involving the Federation would, however, frequently arise in State Courts. The Federal Legislature might, for instance, provide for the taking of proceedings under federal laws in State Courts. In addition, State Courts would have to apply federal law in relation to State law. Article II of the Constitution provides, as any federal Constitution must prescribe, that the Constitution shall be the supreme law of the Federation and of the federated States. Any State law which is inconsistent with it will be invalid; though, in order to limit judicial review where disallowance is provided as the alternative remedy, a State law which might have been disallowed would not be invalid. Similarly, if a State law is inconsistent with a valid federal law, the latter prevails over the former and the former is invalid.

Thus, when a State court is called upon to apply a State law, it might have to determine whether the State law was within the powers of the State, whether there was a federal law covering the same ground, and whether the federal law was valid. If the State court was empowered to apply federal laws, it might have to determine whether those federal laws were valid. The Federal Legislature, on the other hand, might set up special federal courts to determine questions under federal laws, and then those courts would have to decide what federal laws were valid.

For instance, let us suppose that a ship carrying

passengers from Westminster to Southend did not carry safety appliances to satisfy Board of Trade regulations made under the Merchant Shipping Acts, and the owners were charged with an offence. It would be argued by the owners that the regulations, and the provisions of the Acts which authorised them, were invalid. They would have to argue, and the court would have to decide, the very nice point whether Southend was on the sea, as the tag to its name implies, or was on the River Thames. This would be necessary because exclusive power to make laws for shipping "except on inland waterways" is by Article XIX of the (draft) Constitution vested in the Federal Legislature. If, on the other hand, the owners were charged under a *federal* law, they would argue exactly the opposite, that Southend was on the River Thames, an inland waterway. In the one case the court would decide whether the British Act was invalid: in the other it would have to decide whether the federal law was valid. In both cases it would be called upon to interpret the Constitution.

Clearly, the interpretation of the Constitution or of federal laws cannot be left to the State Courts alone. To do so would be to allow different interpretations to be adopted in different States. Accordingly, it is necessary to give a right of appeal to the Federal Supreme Court, as is done by Article XXII, section 2, of the draft. The Supreme Court would then be the final interpreter of the Constitution. Its interpretations of federal laws could be overruled, because the laws could be changed by the Legislature, as is often done in England. Its interpretation of the Constitution could not be overruled by the Federal Legislature, because the Constitution would be as binding on the Federal Legislature as upon any individual or State within the Federation. If the Supreme Court adopted an unfortunate interpretation, only a constitutional amendment could reverse the decision.

§ 2. The Judges.

It is evident that to secure the proper fulfilment of these functions the Federation must draw upon the finest legal talent in the federated States. The judges must be able, they must be as impartial as any judges can be, and they must not be appointed because of their political or social opinions. The example of many States shows that these qualifications are not easily obtained. There is the further difficulty that the States will have widely different legal systems and that few people are aware of the qualifications of lawyers in as many as two States.

To secure impartiality and freedom from political pressure, it is obviously necessary to have judges nominated by an independent body which I have called (Article XXII, section 5) the Judiciary Commission. I suggest further that this body should be appointed by the States' House. I choose that House for two reasons. The first is that the quality of a judge does not depend on the size of the population of his State, and a fair distribution of seats in the Judiciary Commission is more likely from that House than from the People's House. The second is that since the Federal Government is intended to be responsible to the People's House, the States' House is more likely to resist political pressure from the Government. On the other hand, it does not matter that the members of the States' House are more closely associated with the States, because to a large degree the judges must be drawn from the State Courts and the lawyers that practise before them.

The members of the Judiciary Commission should hold office because of their qualifications and not because of their politics. We should expect that the Lord Chancellor or some other person who holds or has held high judicial office would be the British representative. In many continental countries, however, law teachers are regarded as holding the highest legal appointments, so it would be necessary to allow deans of Law Schools to be elected. Members should hold their offices for fixed terms, and I have provided for terms of three years, with a power of re-appointment.

An alternative method of appointment to the Judiciary Commission would be to establish a panel of, say, five persons in each State to nominate for membership. This is, however, a complicated method which might more easily introduce the political element. One must trust somebody somewhere, and I believe that open appointment in the States' House, where any nomination would be open to debate, would be preferable to the backstairs negotiations that might precede nomination of and by a panel in a State.

From time to time, as occasion arose, the Judiciary Commission would nominate judges for appointment by the President. Such judges should hold office for life, or until they reach a retiring age, and their salaries should not be reduced during their tenure of office. These precautions are familiar, and are intended to secure that the judges are as independent as possible of political pressure. At the same time, there must be power to remove an incompetent or corrupt judge, and accordingly I have provided in Article XXII, section 6, that a judge *may* be removed by the President on receiving a resolution to that effect from both Houses of the Federal Legislature. If additional precautions were required, it could be provided that the President should act only at the request of the Judiciary Commission.

I have provided (Article XXII, section 8) that the judges should themselves appoint one of their members to be Chief Justice. He would also be deputy to the President (Article V, section 4) and would determine, if need be, whether a Bill was a Money Bill (Article VII, section 3).

§ 3. Amendment of the Constitution.

The Constitution would provide for the vesting in the Federation of the powers deemed to be necessary, but would leave everything else to the States. It would be the result of long negotiation and close compromise. A State would not enter the Federation unless it felt that its future safety and prosperity were enhanced by membership. In particular, a small State would not enter if it felt that it could be prejudiced by the joint action of other States at a later stage. We are thus faced with a problem which applies to all federations. Any constitution is sure to be defective. Some of the fears of the draftsmen would prove to be groundless, some of their hopes would be blighted. A constitution is drafted according to anticipations which the course of events will nullify. It must be capable of change to meet new conditions, and yet it must not be capable of change to the prejudice of a particular State, for if it is that State probably will not enter. We require an amending power which must not be too easy to operate, lest States fear that, having accepted limitations, they find them increased, or having insisted on precautions, they find them taken away. At the same time, the amending power must not be too difficult to operate, or the Federation will in due course find itself saddled with provisions which prove only to be a nuisance.

Amendment by ordinary legislation is too easy. It may be suitable for a unitary State like the United Kingdom, but it is not suitable for a federation where minorities must be protected. The main protection for the smaller States is that they can, by a combination in the States' House, prevent the power of the larger States in the People's House from overriding their interests. It seems clear, therefore, that no alteration of the proportional representation of a State in the States' House should be made without its consent. In other respects, the smaller States seem to be adequately protected if a two-thirds majority in each House is required. This would require the collaboration of at least twelve States in the States' House—assuming, what is almost incredible, that all the representatives of every State voted on the same side. If this is not a strict enough precaution, it could be provided that in addition two-thirds of the States should consent, and this would require the consent of thirteen States. However, the easier the power of amendment, the more likely the Constitution is to work effectively, provided only that States consider that they have enough protection.

CHAPTER XI

A PRACTICABLE SCHEME?

This chapter is headed by a question because it is for the reader, not the author, to answer it. I have tried to produce a scheme which could, I think, be achieved and which, when achieved, could be worked. Had I been engaged in the delightful task of producing an ideal constitution, it would be very different from that which follows in the Appendix. It is, however, a document prepared to form a basis for discussion. The reader is asked to go into Committee, to pick holes in it and, if he can, fill them, to cut it up into small pieces and put it together again in form as different as he pleases, or, if he thinks fit, to wipe it out altogether and start anew. If he, or I, or anybody else, cannot produce a plan which would be acceptable and work when accepted, then we must expect to see a war in every generation.

Whether some plan of federation proves acceptable depends on the willingness of statesmen to take great decisions. So far as the United Kingdom is concerned, the willingness of statesmen depends on the pressure which people bring upon them. Statesmen on both sides of the House of Commons have spoken about the need for a "new order", for establishing institutions which will affirm and protect the rule of law. The Prime Minister of the French Republic has gone even further, though he, too, has necessarily been vague. Our leaders will lead if they are sure that we will follow. This book has been written in order that the reader may decide for himself whether he would be willing to follow. If he and many others decide to follow, then somebody will be found ready to lead.

I think that I have raised all the important questions that need to be answered. I have given answers, too; but they are not the necessary and inevitable answers. There are probably better answers: they are almost certainly not the answers which would be given by a Constitutional Conference summoned to establish the "new order". All I have attempted to do is to show that there are answers, and to suggest the lines along which they might be found.

This plan, or any plan, involves the surrender by States of some of their cherished rights. It means that, in some part, we must be governed by "foreigners". The fundamental question to be answered is whether we and they are willing, for some purposes, to be governed by representative foreigners whom we shall have some part in choosing, or whether we prefer to keep our sovereignty intact, fighting for it from time to time, and running the risk of not winning. If we lose, we may be governed by "foreigners" indeed—foreigners of the kind who were responsible for the outbreak of the three wars now raging in the world, or even foreigners who regard the present desperadoes as mere amateurs.

I have said that the plan which I have drafted could be worked: I have not said that it would be worked.

Government can be rendered difficult or even impossible by an inappropriate framework; but government is a question of men more than of laws, and no institution will work if men will not work it. All that the draftsman can do is to provide a flexible instrument which is likely to cause the least friction. The nations who should, it is suggested, take part in the Federation are all but one accustomed to the working of democratic institutions. The exception, Germany, is, it is true, the largest of the nations. My original proposal, made publicly in the United States in December, 1938, though drafted immediately after Munich, was for a federation which excluded Germany. It was a means for defending Western civilisation against Nazi barbarism. Yet the Germans have made immense contributions to that civilisation; they are indeed part of it, and they can throw out the barbaric and destructive elements if they are given the opportunity. There is nothing in democracy, difficult as a method of government though it is, which is contrary to the essentially German genius. The Germans would work a federal and democratic system as enthusiastically, as energetically and as efficiently as they—or the rump of them—now follow strange, barbaric gods.

The alternative is to return to the Foch plan of dismembering Germany and seeking to destroy German nationalism. It would not, I think, be permanently successful. It would create a reaction greater than that of 1933. It would not be carried out systematically, because, even if a majority in this country agreed, it would be an unstable majority. At the election after the "Khaki" election, with which this war would end, the minority would probably become a majority, and Great Britain and France would thence follow different paths. If successive French Governments nevertheless continued on the Foch plan, the sympathy of Great Britain, and probably also of many neutrals, would be on the German side. When the reaction appeared in Germany, it would be aimed at France; and Great Britain probably would stand aside.

This is, of course, hypothesis. Possibly the Germans would come under Russian domination. Yet, whatever the course of events, I do not believe that the plan would succeed for long. Federation, it seems to me, is the only possible alternative. It seeks to convert the German menace into German collaboration, and I believe that that collaboration would be whole-hearted once it was perceived that it was genuinely sought and enthusiastically welcomed.

My appeal is, of course, to British people, whose ideals, combined with those which inspired the French Revolution, have had so much influence in the establishment of democracy in Western Europe. The systems operated from the Mediterranean to the Arctic are copies of the British system, adapted by others to meet the varieties of national character and the conditions of national life. The plan in this book is based essentially on the British tradition, as adapted by British people, whether loyalists or rebels, to the conditions of North America and Australia. The question at the head of this chapter is addressed primarily to the peoples of the British Commonwealth, and they ought, more than any, to be ready with a sympathetic answer. It is from them that the initiative must come.

Federation cannot come, however, from British people alone. The collaboration of the French, in the first place, is essential. They, more than anybody, are faced for the third time in three-quarters of a century with the German menace. They, too, have a democratic system. Their publicists seized the essential characteristics of the British Constitution and elaborated out of the misty vagueness of British political thought the clean-cut principles of 1789. It was in that form that they spread across Europe. I have said already that the proposals in this book seek to perpetuate those principles. I hope that this book will be read by French people. Their Prime Minister, as usual, has expressed the same war aims as ours with much greater precision and much greater clarity. Our collaboration for war is close; if the proposals in this book, or anything like them, were accepted, our collaboration for peace would be even closer.

Next, there are what we call the "neutrals". One of them, Finland, is indeed engaged in a war of her own, a war which was thrust upon her by aggression even more obviously than our war was thrust upon Poland. We call them "neutrals" knowing that any one of them, or all of them, may be defending their liberties before these words are in print. The proposal for federation is as much in their interest as it is in ours. They collaborated wholeheartedly in the League of Nations; it was not they who caused it to fail in its major task. They are now living on the sides of two erupting volcanoes. Federation gives them the opportunity to render one extinct and to build an impassable wall against lava from the other—if, indeed, it should continue erupting. Their assistance is essential because they would provide a balance heavy enough to prevent domination by one or two of the more populous States.

Finally, there are the Germans. It is unlikely that these words will be read by any except those who have been compelled to seek a freer atmosphere. To the émigrés nothing more need be said; they have seen naked aggression in action. To the others it is hardly possible to say anything because they cannot listen, and would hardly dare if they could. One sentence is enough. If the proposals of this book were accepted, or any similar proposals were adopted, they would provide an honourable settlement for post-war Europe, under which the immense energy of the German nation could be used for constructive purposes and the best elements of German culture spread around the world.

APPENDIX

Rough Draft of a Proposed Constitution
for a Federation of Western Europe

ARTICLE I

The Federation

1. The Federation of Western Europe (hereinafter called "the Federation") is a federal union composed of such States (hereinafter called "the federated States") as shall have ratified this Constitution in accordance with this Article.

2. Any of the following States shall become a federated State on giving notice to Her Majesty the Queen of the Netherlands that it has ratified this Constitution: the German Reich, Belgium, Denmark, Eire, Finland, the French Republic, the United Kingdom of Great Britain and Northern Ireland, Iceland, the Grand Duchy of Luxemburg, the Kingdom of the Netherlands, Norway, Sweden and the Swiss Confederation.

3. Subsequent provisions of this Constitution shall take effect from the date when four of the States mentioned in section 2 of this Article have given notice of ratification, and for the purposes of this Constitution "the establishment of the Federation" is that date: provided that, where a State ratifies this Constitution after that date, this Constitution shall apply to that State as from the date of such ratification.

4. A federated State named in section 2 of this Article may not be expelled from the Federation nor shall it withdraw from the Federation, except by an amendment of this Constitution.

5. Any of the following shall become a federated

State on giving notice of ratification to Her Majesty the Queen of the Netherlands: the Dominion of Canada, the Commonwealth of Australia, the Union of South Africa, the Dominion of New Zealand, Newfoundland and Southern Rhodesia: provided that

(A) Newfoundland shall not become a federated State until it has become self-governing.

(B) Nothing in this Constitution shall forbid the union of Southern Rhodesia with Northern Rhodesia, or any part thereof, and the united territory shall succeed to the rights and duties of Southern Rhodesia as a federated State under this Constitution.

(C) Except where a contrary intention appears, nothing in this Constitution shall affect the relations *inter se* of the members of the British Commonwealth of Nations.

(D) Any federated State named in this section of this Article may withdraw from the Federation one year after giving notice to the President of its intention so to do.

6. Other States may be admitted to the Federation, on such conditions as may be prescribed, by a law assented to by at least two-thirds of the whole number of members in each House of the Federal Legislature [and approved by the legislatures in at least two-thirds of the federated States?]; such States shall then become federated States.

7. The Federal Legislature may, by a law assented to by at least two-thirds of the whole number of members in each House, extend to any State, not being a federated State, at the request of such State, any of the provisions of this Constitution; and for the purposes of such

provision only such State shall be deemed to be a federated State.

8. Except where the contrary intention appears, "State" in this Constitution includes the dependencies of the State, and "dependency" includes a colony, a protected State, a protectorate, a territory in respect of which a mandate on behalf of the League of Nations has been accepted by the State or the head thereof, and any other country or territory under the protection or suzerainty of a State or the head thereof.

ARTICLE II

THE CONSTITUTION AS SUPREME LAW

This Constitution shall be the supreme law of the Federation and of the federated States and shall override such laws, whether constitutional or otherwise, of a federated State as are inconsistent with it: provided that a State law shall not be deemed to be invalid merely because it is contrary to the provisions of this Constitution if the President had in respect of that law a power of disallowance.

ARTICLE III

FEDERAL GUARANTEE TO STATES

The Federation guarantees the territorial integrity of each federated State, undertakes to protect the democratic system of every such State and, subject to this

Constitution, undertakes to assist each federated State in the maintenance of public order within the State: provided that

(A) Nothing in this Constitution shall prevent boundary changes by agreement between the federated States concerned.
(B) The Federal Legislature may, at the request of a federated State, authorise the division of that State into two or more States, and may amend this Constitution accordingly.
(C) Nothing in this Constitution shall prevent the grant by the Federation or by a federated State to a dependency controlled by the Federation or the State, as the case may be, of self-government; and such dependency may be admitted into the Federation as a federated State in accordance with section 5 of Article I of this Constitution.

ARTICLE IV

CITIZENSHIP

1. In this Constitution a reference to citizens of a State shall be taken to include a reference to subjects of that State or its monarch.

2. All citizens of the federated States shall also be citizens of the Federation, and are hereinafter referred to as "federal citizens" provided that, British subjects who are citizens or nationals of a British Dominion which is not a federated State or who, being domiciled in a British Dominion which is not a federated State, do not indicate to the Government of that Dominion within one year from the establishment of the Federation that

they wish to become federal citizens, shall not be federal citizens.

3. Persons belonging to a dependency of a federated State who are not federal citizens shall be federal protected persons.

4. The Federal Legislature shall have exclusive power to make laws for the issue of passports to federal citizens and federal protected persons and for the protection of such persons outside the Federation.

5. Federal citizens within a federated State, not being citizens of that State, shall have the same rights and duties as citizens of that State: provided that the laws of the State may

(A) Exclude such federal citizens from all or any of the rights and duties directly associated with the operation of the political institutions of that State; and
(B) Prescribe a reasonable period of residence before any right or any duty of any such federal citizen shall accrue.

ARTICLE V

THE PRESIDENT

1. On the establishment of the Federation, Her Majesty the Queen of the Netherlands shall appoint a person to be Acting President of the Federation.

2. As soon as may be after the first meeting of the Federal Legislature and thereafter as soon as may be after the office of President falls vacant, the two Houses of the Federal Legislature, meeting in joint session, shall elect a person as President of the Federation.

3. The President shall hold office for three years but may be re-elected, and may resign by message addressed to both Houses of the Federal Legislature.

4. Whenever the office of President is vacant or the President is unable to act by reason of illness, absence or otherwise, the Chief Justice of the Federal Supreme Court shall be Acting President; and in this Constitution a reference to "President" means the President of the Federation or the Acting President.

5. Except where the contrary is expressly stated, the powers of the President under this Constitution shall be exercised by the President at the request of the Council of Ministers.

6. The legislature of a federated State may enact laws for determining the precedence and the immunities of the President in that State, but legal proceedings in respect of any act of the President in his official capacity may not be brought except in a federal court.

ARTICLE VI

THE COUNCIL OF MINISTERS

1. When the office of Prime Minister is vacant, the President may, in his discretion, appoint such person to be Prime Minister as he thinks fit.

2. The Prime Minister may resign by writing addressed to the President, and he may be dismissed by the President (who shall act in his discretion) if a resolution requesting the President so to do has been passed by the People's House.

3. Other ministers shall be appointed by the President at the request of the Prime Minister, and such of these ministers as the Prime Minister indicates shall be members of the Council of Ministers, of which the Prime Minister shall be chairman.

4. The Prime Minister and the other ministers shall be, or within six months after appointment shall become, members of the one or the other House of the Federal Legislature.

ARTICLE VII

The Federal Legislature

1. The legislative power of the Federation shall be vested in two Houses, the People's House and the States' House.

2. A Bill assented to by a majority in each House shall become law on being signed by the President:

Provided that a money Bill assented to by the People's House and rejected by the States' House, or assented to by the States' House with amendments which are rejected by the People's House, or not assented to by the States' House within three months of its receipt by the States' House, on again being assented to by the People's House without further amendment (excepting only such amendments as have been accepted by the States' House) and being signed by the President shall become law without being assented to by the States' House.

3. For the purposes of this Article a money Bill is a

Bill which is certified by the Chief Justice of the Federal Supreme Court for the time being to be a Bill which contains only provisions dealing with all or any of the following subjects, namely:

(A) The imposition, repeal, remission, alteration or regulation of taxation.
(B) The raising or guarantee of any federal loan or the repayment thereof.
(C) The expenditure of money on services already authorised by the laws of the Federation.

ARTICLE VIII

MEETING AND DISSOLUTION OF THE FEDERAL LEGISLATURE

1. The first meeting of the Federal Legislature shall be held as soon as may be after the establishment of the Federation, on a date to be fixed by proclamation issued by the Acting President.

2. The Federal Legislature may be dissolved by proclamation issued by the President, and such proclamation shall order new elections and shall fix a date for the first meeting of the new Legislature. The President shall not issue a proclamation under this section except at the request of the Council of Ministers; but he may, in his discretion and subject to section 3 of this Article, refuse to issue such a proclamation.

3. Such a proclamation must be issued before the expiry of five years from the date of the first meeting of the Legislature being dissolved: provided that the

Federal Legislature may prolong this period for one year and no longer.

4. Where a State accedes to the Federation after the establishment of the Federation, the President shall as soon as may be by proclamation order elections in that State for members of both Houses and (in the absence of a federal law to the contrary) the State legislature shall enact the laws necessary for this purpose.

5. Casual vacancies in either House shall be notified to that House by the President and shall be filled in the manner provided by this Constitution for the election of members to that House.

ARTICLE IX

THE PEOPLE'S HOUSE

1. The People's House shall be composed of members elected by the people of the Federation.

2. The number of members elected from each federal State shall be in proportion to the number of federal electors in that State; and, until the Federal Legislature otherwise provides, each State shall have one member for every 500,000 federal electors: provided that a federated State shall have at least as many members in the People's House as it has in the States' House.

3. The Federal Legislature shall have exclusive power to determine the qualifications of federal electors and of members of the People's House, the electoral areas for the election of members to that House, and the methods of election. Subject to section 2 of this Article,

it shall also have power to determine the number of members of the People's House.

4. Until the Federal Legislature otherwise provides, the federal electors in any federated State shall be the persons entitled to elect members to the most numerous House of the State legislature: provided that

(A) For the purpose of section 2 of this Article, the number of federal electors in any federated State shall be the number of persons entitled to elect members to the most numerous House of the State legislature at the establishment of the Federation, and the number shall not thereafter be altered for the purposes of that section until the Federal Legislature so provides; and

(B) A federal elector shall not have more than one vote in each electoral area unless the Federal Legislature otherwise provides.

5. Until the Federal Legislature otherwise provides:

(1) Each federal State shall form a single area for the election of members, and the elections shall be conducted on the principle of proportional representation with a single transferable vote; but the State legislature may, with the consent of the Council of Ministers, divide the State into two or more areas for the purpose of the election of members.

(2) Any federal elector may be elected a member.

(3) The conduct of federal elections in any federated State shall be under the control and at the expense of the State, and the State legislature shall enact laws accordingly; but such laws may be disallowed by the President.

6. In this Article "State" does not include the dependencies of that State but, in the case of a federated State in Europe, does include all the territories of that State in Europe (including Greenland).

ARTICLE X

THE STATES' HOUSE

1. The States' House shall consist of members from each federated State elected in accordance with the provisions of State laws enacted for that purpose.

2. The number of members from each federated State shall be a follows:

The German Reich	9 members
The French Republic and the United Kingdom of Great Britain and Northern Ireland	7 members each
The Commonwealth of Australia, Belgium, the Dominion of Canada, Denmark, Eire, Finland, the Kingdom of the Netherlands, New Zealand, Norway, the Union of South Africa, Sweden and the Swiss Confederation	5 members each
Iceland, the Grand Duchy of Luxemburg, Newfoundland and Southern Rhodesia	3 members each

3. The Federal Legislature may, by law assented to by at least two-thirds of the whole number of members in each House, provide for the representation in the States' House of any State to which section 7 of Article I of this Constitution applies, or of any State which is, or is qualified to be elected, a member of the League of Nations: provided that the representatives from any such State shall have a right to speak but not to vote. Where under this Constitution a certain proportion of the whole number of members of the States' House is

required for any purpose, members of the States' House under this section shall be excluded for the purpose of calculating such proportion.

ARTICLE XI

GENERAL LEGISLATIVE POWER

1. The Federal Legislature shall have power to make such laws as may be necessary and proper for carrying into execution the powers of the Federation or of the Federal Legislature or other federal institution or officer under this Constitution.

2. The Federal Legislature shall have power to authorise the application of federal funds for the general welfare of the Federation.

3. The powers not exclusively vested in the Federal Legislature by this Constitution nor withdrawn by it from the federated States may continue to be exercised by the federated States; but when a law of a State is inconsistent with a law of the Federation the latter shall prevail and the former shall, to the extent of the inconsistency, be invalid.

4. In this Constitution, "rights" include powers, privileges and immunities, and "duties" include liabilities.

ARTICLE XII

Disallowance of State Legislation

1. Where under this Constitution the President has a power to disallow State legislation he shall have power also to disallow administrative acts of the same character; and such power may be exercised within a period of three months from the enactment of the legislation or the coming into operation of the administrative act. Any such disallowance shall be notified by the President by proclamation, and the legislation or administrative act shall, from the date of the proclamation, cease to be law.

2. Without prejudice to other powers set out in this Constitution, the President shall have power to disallow any law of a federated State which, in the opinion of the Council of Ministers,

(A) Tends to interfere with the freedom of elections to the People's House; or
(B) Tends to prevent the formation or constitutional operation of political parties having federal objects; or
(C) Is likely to require the performance by the Federation of its obligations under Article III of this Constitution.

ARTICLE XIII

External Relations

1. The conduct of relations between the Federation and States not members of the Federation shall be vested in the President and, subject to this Article, no federated

State shall have relations with States not members of the Federation.

2. The Federal Legislature shall have power to prescribe the subjects on which any federated State may make treaties or otherwise contract obligations or enter into relations with States not members of the Federation; and, until the Federal Legislature so provides, such treaties, obligations or relations may extend to any matter not within the exclusive competence of the Federal Legislature nor withdrawn by this Constitution from the competence of a State. A treaty or other arrangement under this section (other than a treaty or arrangement between a federated State which is a member of the British Commonwealth of Nations and a member of the British Commonwealth of Nations that is not a federated State) shall not be valid or binding on a federated State unless it has been signed or ratified on behalf of the President as well as signed or ratified on behalf of the federated State.

3. So long as a treaty or other arrangement under section 2 of this Article is in operation, the Federal Legislature shall have power to enact such laws as may be necessary to give effect to such treaty or arrangement.

4. The obligations of a federated State arising under a treaty or other arrangement made with a State not a member of the Federation before the establishment of the Federation shall, in so far as it deals with matters within the exclusive competence of the Federal Legislature, become at the establishment of the Federation the obligations of the Federation; and, in so far as it deals

with matters not within the exclusive competence of the Federal Legislature, but not withdrawn from the competence of the federated State, section 3 of this Article shall apply. Obligations of a federated State dealing with matters not within the competence either of the Federal Legislature or of the federated State shall be deemed to be extinguished.

5. The obligations of the United Kingdom of Great Britain and Northern Ireland in respect of the defence of other members of the British Commonwealth of Nations shall be deemed to arise under an "arrangement" for the purposes of this Article.

ARTICLE XIV

RELATIONS BETWEEN FEDERATED STATES

1. A federated State may make treaties or otherwise contract obligations with any other federated State in relation to matters which are not within the exclusive competence of the federated State nor withdrawn by this Constitution from the competence of the federated State, but such treaties or arrangements shall be of no effect unless they are signed or ratified on behalf of the President as well as signed or ratified on behalf of the federated State.

2. Where the treaty or arrangement under section 1 of this Article so provides, the Federal Legislature shall have power to make laws to give effect to the treaty or other arrangement or any part of it.

3. Treaties and other arrangements between federated States in operation at the establishment of the Federation shall continue in force until they are abrogated in accordance with their terms, or until they are declared by the Federal Legislature to be inconsistent with this Constitution.

ARTICLE XV

DEFENCE

1. The command of the armed forces of the Federation shall be vested in the President.

2. From such a date as may be fixed by the Federal Legislature, the armed forces of the federated State, or such of them as may be indicated by the Federal Legislature, shall be transferred to the President and shall become part of the armed forces of the Federation. Within twelve months of that date, armed forces of any federated State not so transferred shall be disbanded and, subject to this Constitution, no federated State or authority or person shall establish or maintain armed forces within the Federation: provided that a federated State may authorise the establishment or maintenance of such police forces as may be necessary for the maintenance of order within its own boundaries.

3. From the establishment of the Federation, no arms, munitions, military equipment or other implements of war shall be manufactured in or imported into the Federation except under the licence of the President.

4. The President shall, at the request of the appropriate authority in a federated State, authorise the armed forces of the Federation to assist the State authority in the enforcement of the laws of the federated State and the maintenance of order in the federated State.

5. In section 2 of this Article, "armed forces" includes the arms, equipment, munitions and other implements of war, and the land and buildings used exclusively for defence purposes.

6. Laws of any State which, in the opinion of the Council of Ministers, are inconsistent with this Article may be disallowed by the President.

ARTICLE XVI

DEPENDENCIES

1. There shall be established a Colonial Commission to exercise the functions conferred upon it by this Constitution and by laws made by the Federal Legislature.

2. The Colonial Commission shall consist of such number of persons having, subject to this Article, such qualifications, as may be provided by the Federal Legislature. Members shall be appointed by the President on the nomination of the two Houses of the Federal Legislature, acting by joint resolution, and shall not be members of either House of the Federal Legislature, nor hold any other office of profit in the Federation

or in any federated State. Each member shall hold office for six years, but may be reappointed, and may be removed by the President if a resolution to that effect is passed by both Houses of the Federal Legislature. He shall have such salary as may be prescribed by federal law, but it may not be reduced during his term of office.

3. By agreement with any federated State, the Federal Legislature may provide for the transfer to the Federation of any rights which the federated State exercises in any dependency. Inhabitants of the dependency shall not thereby lose their citizenship, but the Federal Legislature may provide for the conferment of federal citizenship upon other inhabitants and, in so far as they are not federal citizens, the inhabitants shall be federal protected persons.

4. Where rights are transferred to the Federation under section 3 of this Article the Federal Legislature shall have exclusive power to make laws for the exercise of such rights.

5. In so far as the rights of a federated State are not transferred to the Federation under section 3 of this Article, they shall be exercised subject to the following restrictions:

(A) They shall be exercised for the well-being and development of the people of the dependency.
(B) The laws in force in the dependency shall not discriminate between federated States or the citizens of federated States, but shall apply to the citizens of any other federated State as they apply to the citizens of the federated State exercising such rights: provided that this restriction shall not prevent the federated

State from prescribing an official language or official languages.

(c) Appointments to the governmental services of the dependency shall be open to the citizens of other federated States as they are open to the citizens of the federated State exercising such rights: provided that the federated State may impose a language qualification.

(d) The federated State exercising such rights shall make an annual report to the Colonial Commission on the condition of the dependency.

6. If the Colonial Commission reports that, in its opinion, any law is contrary to the provisions of section 5 of this Article, the President may disallow such law. The Colonial Commission shall have a similar power in respect of laws in force at the establishment of the Federation, but such power shall be exercised, if at all, within twelve months of the establishment of the Federation.

7. Without prejudice to the generality of section 2 of Article XI, the Federal Legislature shall have power, if the Colonial Commission so recommends, to make grants, on such conditions as may be prescribed by the Legislature, to assist a federated State in the development of the well-being of the inhabitants of any dependency.

8. If the Colonial Commission so recommends, the Federal Legislature may authorise a federated State to establish and maintain in a dependency, under such conditions as the law may provide, such armed forces as are, in the opinion of the Colonial Commission, neces-

sary for the maintenance of order in the dependency and for the protection of any frontiers of the dependency that do not abut on the territory of, or on territory occupied by, the Federation or a federated State.

9. If the Colonial Commission so recommends, the President shall withdraw from a federated State, for a period recommended by the Colonial Commission, such assistance in the maintenance of order in a dependency as may have been granted under Article XV of this Constitution.

10. The Colonial Commission shall make an annual report, and such other reports as may be deemed necessary, to the President, and such reports shall be laid before both Houses of the Federal Legislature.

ARTICLE XVII

MOST-FAVOURED NATION

1. On the establishment of the Federation, each federated State shall be deemed to have granted to every other federated State and its citizens, in any matter relating to trade, commerce, shipping, navigation, air traffic, and industry, every privilege, favour or immunity whatever which such State may have granted before the establishment of the Federation to any other State, whether federated or not, or to the citizens of any such State; and the laws of the State shall be deemed to have been amended accordingly.

2. This Article shall apply to privileges granted to a

British Dominion or to any dependency of a State, as it applies to a State.

3. This Article shall not impose on Belgium the obligation of extending to other federated States the privileges granted to Luxemburg, nor impose on Luxemburg the obligation of extending to other federated States the privileges granted to Belgium; and for the purposes of this Article Belgium and Luxemburg shall be considered to be one federated State.

ARTICLE XVIII*

INTER-STATE TRADE AND MIGRATION

1. At the expiration of a period of ten years from the establishment of the Federation all laws of any federated State restricting commerce between federated States shall, subject to this Constitution, cease to have effect, and thereafter commerce between federated States shall, subject to this Constitution, be free.

2. In this Constitution, "commerce" includes all movements of commodities across the boundaries and through the ports of a federated State.

3. The provisions of this Article shall not forbid the making of laws by a federated State designed only

(A) To prevent the spread of disease, whether in human beings, animals, birds, fish or plants.

---

* See the Supplementary Articles XVIIIA and XIXA which, if adopted, would supersede Articles XVIII to XXI.

(B)   To prevent the carriage of narcotics, poisons, dangerous articles, or obscene or blasphemous literature.

(C)   To prevent the entry into any federated State of persons who have been convicted, or have been charged and not acquitted, of crime in any State, whether federated or not.

(D)   To regulate the frontier posts or ports through which commerce or the movement of persons may be permitted.

(E)   To enable the federated State to control the production, supply or distribution of any commodity within the State: provided that such a law shall not exclude or substantially interfere with commerce with any other federated State.

4. Any such law as is mentioned in section 3 of this Article may be disallowed by the President; but the federated State may refer the law so disallowed to the Federal Supreme Court and, if the Court decides that the law so referred was designed only to effect one or more of the purposes mentioned in section 3 of this Article the disallowance shall operate as a suspension only, and the law shall take effect on a date fixed by the federated State, not being a date earlier than the date of the decision of the Court.

5. The Federal Legislature shall have exclusive power to regulate the migration of persons to and from the territories in Europe of federated States. A federated State within section 2 of this Article shall have power to make laws relating to migration in respect of its dependencies, but such laws may be disallowed by the President on the advice of the Colonial Commission; and laws relating to migration in respect of such dependencies

in force at the establishment of the Federation may be repealed by the Federal Legislature.

6. The laws of a federated State within section 5 of Article I of this Constitution shall not, in so far as they relate to migration, discriminate between federal citizens from different federated States in Europe.

ARTICLE XIX*

EXTERNAL TRADE

1. After the expiration of a period of ten years from the establishment of the Federation, the Federal Legislature shall have exclusive power to make laws relating to

(A) Trade and commerce between the Federation and countries or territories outside the Federation.
(B) Navigation and shipping, except on the inland waterways of a federated State.
(C) Traffic by air.

2. In the exercise of powers under this Article the Federation shall not by law or administrative act give preference to one federated State or any part thereof over another federated State or any part thereof.

* See the note to Article XVIII.

*ARTICLE XX**

OTHER ECONOMIC POWERS

1. The Federal Legislature shall have power to make laws relating to

(A) Currency, coinage and legal tender.
(B) Banking, inter-State payments and the transfer of securities.
(C) Weights and measures.

2. In the exercise of any power under this Article the Federal Legislature shall be entitled to declare that its power is exclusive.

*ARTICLE XXI**

TRADE; TRANSITIONAL

1. Until a period of ten years from the establishment of the Federation has elapsed, a federated State shall have full power to make laws relating to trade and commerce, shipping and navigation, and traffic by air.

2. Laws made under section 1 of this Article shall not give preference to one federated State or a part thereof over another federated State or a part thereof.

3. Any law made under this Article may be dis-

* See the note to Article XVIII.

allowed by the President if, in the opinion of the Council of Ministers, it

(A) Gives a preference contrary to section 2 of this Article; or
(B) Substantially increases the difficulties of trade and commerce within the Federation.

ARTICLE XXII

THE FEDERAL JUDICIARY

1. There shall be a Federal Supreme Court which shall have original and exclusive jurisdiction in

(A) All disputes between any two or more federated States.
(B) All disputes between a federated State or federated States and the Federation.
(C) Prize.
(D) Piracy on the high seas; and
(E) Such other matters within the competence of the Federal Legislature as that legislature may prescribe.

2. The Federal Supreme Court shall have appellate jurisdiction in all cases concerning the interpretation of this Constitution and of all legislation made by the Federal Legislature.

3. The Federal Legislature shall have exclusive power to create such inferior tribunals with such jurisdiction as it thinks fit for the administration of the laws of the Federation.

4. The Federal Legislature shall have exclusive power to make laws for the exercise of jurisdiction under this Article by federal courts and tribunals.

5. The judges of the Federal Supreme Court shall be appointed by the President on the nomination of a Judiciary Commission. The members of the Judiciary Commission shall be appointed by the States' House and shall be persons who hold or have held high judicial office in the Federation or in any federated State, or persons who hold or have held the office of dean of a Law Faculty, or similar office, in any University in any federated State. A member of the Judiciary Commission shall hold office for three years, but may be reappointed, and may resign by notice in writing to the President, who shall communicate such notice to the States' House.

6. A judge of the Federal Supreme Court shall hold office for life:

Provided that

(A) The Federal Legislature shall have power to make laws fixing an age for the retirement of judges.

(B) A judge may resign on giving notice in writing to the President, who shall communicate it to the Judiciary Commission.

(C) A judge may be removed by the President on receiving a resolution to that effect from both Houses of the Federal Legislature.

7. The salary of a judge shall be fixed by the Federal Legislature, but shall not be diminished during his tenure of office.

8. The judges of the Federal Supreme Court shall appoint one of their number to be Chief Justice of the Federal Supreme Court, and he shall hold office until he ceases to be a judge of the Federal Supreme Court, or resigns the office.

ARTICLE XXIII

AMENDMENTS TO THIS CONSTITUTION

Amendments to this Constitution may be prepared in either House, and any such amendment shall take effect if it is supported by at least two-thirds of the members voting in each House [and by a majority in the legislatures of two-thirds of the federated States?]: provided that the proportional representation of a federated State in the States' House shall not be diminished without the consent of the legislature of that State, nor shall this Article be so amended as to enable the proportional representation of a federated State in the States' House to be diminished without the consent of the legislature of that State.

SUPPLEMENTARY ARTICLES

(These Articles, if adopted, would replace
Articles XVIII to XXI)

ARTICLE XVIIIA

CONCURRENT ECONOMIC POWERS

1. The Federal Legislature shall have power to make laws relating to

(A) Trade and commerce between the federated States and between the Federation and foreign countries or territories.
(B) Postal, telegraphic, wireless and other forms of communication.
(C) Currency, coinage and legal tender.
(D) Banking, inter-State payments and the transfer of securities.
(E) Negotiable instruments.
(F) The incorporation and operation of companies.
(G) Bankruptcy and insolvency.
(H) Patents, trade-marks and trade-designs.
(I) Copyright.
(J) Weights and measures.

2. In this Article "commerce" includes the production, transport and distribution of commodities and the provision of services ancillary to commerce, but does not include matters relating only to public safety, public health or conditions of labour: provided that nothing in this definition shall prevent the exercise by the Federal Legislature of powers under section 2 of Article XI.

3. Any law of a State relating to matters within the powers of the Federal Legislature under this Article may be disallowed by the President.

ARTICLE XIX$_A$

EXCLUSIVE ECONOMIC POWERS

1. The Federal Legislature shall have exclusive power to make laws relating to

(A) Navigation and shipping, except on the inland waterways of a federated State.
(B) Traffic by air.
(C) The migration of persons to and from the territories in Europe of federated States.

2. The express mention of subjects in this Article shall not be taken to restrict the definition of "commerce" in section 2 of Article XVIII A which shall, nevertheless, not include matters within this Article.

3. A federated State within section 2 of Article I of this Constitution shall have power to make laws relating to migration to and from its dependencies, but such laws may be disallowed by the President on the advice of the Colonial Commission, and laws relating to migration to and from such dependencies in operation at the establishment of the Federation may be repealed by the Federal Legislature.

4. The laws of a federated State within section 5 of Article I of this Constitution shall not, in so far as they relate to migration, discriminate between federal citizens from different federated States in Europe.

INDEX